T0323998

Cambridge Elements ☰

Elements in the Renaissance
edited by
John Henderson
Birkbeck, University of London, and Wolfson College,
University of Cambridge
Jonathan K. Nelson
Syracuse University Florence

WHO OWNS LITERATURE?

Early Modernity's Orphaned Texts

Jane Tylus
Yale University

CAMBRIDGE
UNIVERSITY PRESS

Shaftesbury Road, Cambridge CB2 8EA, United Kingdom

One Liberty Plaza, 20th Floor, New York, NY 10006, USA

477 Williamstown Road, Port Melbourne, VIC 3207, Australia

314–321, 3rd Floor, Plot 3, Splendor Forum, Jasola District Centre,
New Delhi – 110025, India

103 Penang Road, #05–06/07, Visioncrest Commercial, Singapore 238467

Cambridge University Press is part of Cambridge University Press & Assessment,
a department of the University of Cambridge.

We share the University's mission to contribute to society through the pursuit of
education, learning and research at the highest international levels of excellence.

www.cambridge.org
Information on this title: www.cambridge.org/9781009539197

DOI: 10.1017/9781009357876

© Jane Tylus 2024

This publication is in copyright. Subject to statutory exception and to the provisions
of relevant collective licensing agreements, no reproduction of any part may take
place without the written permission of Cambridge University Press & Assessment.

When citing this work, please include a reference to the DOI 10.1017/9781009357876

First published 2024

A catalogue record for this publication is available from the British Library

ISBN 978-1-009-53919-7 Hardback
ISBN 978-1-009-35786-9 Paperback
ISSN 2631-9101 (online)
ISSN 2631-9098 (print)

Cambridge University Press & Assessment has no responsibility for the persistence
or accuracy of URLs for external or third-party internet websites referred to in this
publication and does not guarantee that any content on such websites is, or will
remain, accurate or appropriate.

Who Owns Literature?

Early Modernity's Orphaned Texts

Elements in the Renaissance

DOI: 10.1017/9781009357876
First published online: December 2024

Jane Tylus
Yale University

Author for correspondence: Jane Tylus, jane.tylus@yale.edu

Abstract: Interest in material culture has produced a rigorous body of scholarship that considers the dynamics of licensing, permissions, and patronage – an ongoing history of the estrangement of works from their authors. Additionally, translation studies is enabling new ways to think about the emergence of European vernaculars and the reappropriation of classical and early Christian texts. This Element emerges from these intersecting stories. How did early modern authors say goodbye to their works; how do translators and editors articulate their duty to the dead or those incapable of caring for their work; what happens once censorship is invoked in the name of other forms of protection? The notion of the work as orphan, sent out and unable to return to its author, will take us from Horace to Dante, Montaigne, Anne Bradstreet, and others as we reflect on the relevance of the vocabularies of loss, charity, and licence for literature.

Keywords: translation, editing, early modernity, book history, ownership

© Jane Tylus 2024

ISBNs: 9781009539197 (HB), 9781009357869 (PB), 9781009357876 (OC)
ISSNs: 2631-9101 (online), 2631-9098 (print)

Contents

Prologue

> I believe that books, once they are written, have no need of their authors.[1]
>
> Elena Ferrante, letter to Sandra, 21 September 1991

So wrote the woman known as Elena Ferrante after negotiating the publication of her first novel, *L'amore molesto*. More than three decades later, Ferrante still has not disclosed her real name or identity, and her refusal to give interviews, receive awards, or budge from her insistence that she's 'already done enough for this long story' remains absolute. Yet as apparently commonsensical if today extremely rare her claim might be, one word stands out: *need*. Ferrante contests a general assumption that a book can't exist without its author, that it's a fragile being, at risk if left alone – a sentiment that goes back at least to Plato.[2] Is it a coincidence that a more recent work by Ferrante has the word 'abandoned' in its title, or that her fourth and final Neapolitan novel is about a lost child?

Is Ferrante right? Can books survive without their parent? The following pages will attempt to document the hold of such a question on the early modern imagination through a handful of examples ranging from ancient Rome to late seventeenth-century Mexico. The seemingly harsh words of a brash sixteen-year-old who would become one of the Renaissance's most rigorous humanists, Angelo Poliziano, constitute the first such example. In sentiment they seem no different from Ferrante's verdict. Uttered in the form of a brusque Latin epigram, Poliziano's judgement of a fellow poet goes like this:

> I recently criticized the poems that you had composed, and yet it wasn't actually your poetry that I criticized, Paul. You were the author, I admit, but once they've been published or sent out (edita), poems belong not to the author, but to the public (Auctoris non sunt carmina, sed populi).[3]

Time has effaced our knowledge of Paul, but not of Poliziano himself, as though to prove him right: the apparently bad poems of a fellow writer now belong to others. Or more accurately, they once did; and now we know of their existence only from Poliziano. Chances are they weren't published in the sense that we think of that word today.[4] When Poliziano was writing these lines in the early 1470s, the business of publishing was, at least in Italy, still in its infancy. Paul's

---

[1] Ferrante 2016, p. 3.

[2] In the *Phaedrus*, a written text is liable to being misunderstood: 'when it is ill-treated or unjustly reviled it always needs its father to help it; for it has no power to protect or help itself'; Plato 2005, *Phaedrus* 275e, p. 567. For Plato's metaphor of the author as parent, see McDonald 1993, p. 309.

[3] Poliziano 2019, pp. 30–1.

[4] 'Publication' was a term long before print, as Riddy 2004 reminds us: '*Pubblishen* in middle English means "announce," "proclaim," "divulge," "spread abroad," quite different from one of the OED definitions of "to publish": "to issue or cause to be issued for sale to the public"' (p. 41).

poems were evidently circulated if not published, or more precisely, they were given out; the infinitive form of the verb, *edere*, has its origins in ex + dare. As a result, the poems are no longer his.[5]

But if Poliziano sounds cavalier in his chiding response to Paul, he comes across as even more ruthless with respect to his own work. In a letter that would eventually be used as a preface to the first publication (in the modern sense) of his play *Fabula di Orfeo*, Poliziano addresses one Carlo Canale, a courtier from Mantua, with this grim account:

> History tells us, my dear sir Carlo, that the Lacedaemonians held the follow-
> ing custom: whenever any child of theirs was born with a malformed limb or
> wanting in strength, it was promptly exposed: it could not be kept alive, for
> such stock was deemed unworthy of Lacedaemon. Likewise, I wanted my
> Orpheus play – which was composed at the behest of our most reverend
> Cardinal of Mantua, in two days' time, in the midst of continuous upheaval,
> and in the vulgar language [Italian] such that it would be better understood by
> its spectators – I wanted it promptly, and not unlike Orpheus himself, torn
> apart: for I knew that my daughter would more readily bring her father shame
> before honor, and melancholy before pleasure.[6]

Spartan children born unhealthy or with disabilities are abandoned on mountain-tops to be torn apart by beasts and birds – analogous to the fate Orpheus suffers at the hands of the Bacchanti at the end of Poliziano's play.[7] Commissioned by the Gonzaga family around 1480, the *Orfeo* was composed in the *volgare* or vernacu-lar tongue, possibly one reason for Poliziano's disdain (another might be that he wrote it in a mere two days – no doubt an exaggeration). But Canale evidently persuaded Poliziano to let him indulge in some degree of fatherly affection. Yielding to Canale's misplaced compassion, which Poliziano judges to be little more than 'cruelty', Poliziano consents to his daughter's handoff to others: 'So let her live, since you find her so pleasing' ('Viva adunque, poi che a voi così piace').[8] Yet he also asks that this *figliuola* not be linked to her progenitor, urging Canale to defend him from anyone who 'wanted to attribute the imperfections of such a daughter to her father'.

Cast off as an orphan, the *Fabula di Orfeo* was left exposed to die until she was rescued thanks to another's *pietà*. The preface tellingly contrasts with the ensuing play, about the refusal to let a loved one go. Unable to accept his wife's death, Orpheus descends to hell to charm a tyrant with his song, winning Eurydice back.

---

[5] Van Groningen 1963 for various meanings of the Greek ἐχδοσις.

[6] Poliziano, *The Fable of Orpheus*, trans. J. Perna, unpublished translation (2009), p. 1.

[7] The language used to describe the sickly or malformed in early modernity is discussed in Bearden 2019.

[8] Poliziano, *The Fable of Orpheus*, trans. J. Perna, p. 1; Poliziano 2000, p. 136.

But he must respect one seemingly simple rule: don't turn around to look at her until you're back on earth. Orpheus disobeys, and the heretofore silent Eurydice announces her definitive return to Pluto's realm with a line that resonates in light of both Poliziano's sober announcement to Paul and his letter to Canale: 'né sono hormai più tua':[9] I am no longer yours. Or as Virgil put it in his fourth *Georgic*, one of Poliziano's sources: 'non tua.'[10] We cannot be too attached to what we love – our child, our partner, our work – and must be willing to let go for them to have any kind of life (or death) of their own. And yet perhaps there's another tale here as well, one that Poliziano will return to in a later, Latin text, *Nutricia*. Here he blames not Orfeo for his backward turn (if he could even be said to blame him in the *Fabula*) but Pluto. The 'excessive severity of [his] harsh law' does nothing less than condemn humanity itself.[11] If texts need protection in a hostile world, the poet needs protection too – a poet who can be torn apart as easily as the orphaned work.[12]

These dynamics are all the more interesting insofar as Poliziano himself was an orphan. Following the assassination of his father, a leading political figure in Montepulciano – 'Politian' or 'Poliziano' alludes to his native seat – the ten-year-old boy was sent soon thereafter to a cousin's family in Florence, of lesser economic means than his own. Poliziano's earliest epigrams – aside from his retort to Paul – allude to his poverty; he directs himself at one point to Lorenzo de' Medici asking him to stop praising his poetry and send him some clothes instead![13] The slightly older Lorenzo took him in and facilitated his studies of Greek in the Florentine Studio, where eventually Poliziano would teach. Despite these early successes, as Davide Puccini has mused, 'It's unimaginable that the tragic murder of his father had not left a trace on the soul of the adolescent'. Puccini goes on to suggest that although Poliziano remained silent throughout his life about the event, it's not hard to see in his perennial insecurity the trauma of early loss.[14] Was Poliziano's seemingly calloused attitude about his relationship to his works – and others' relationships to theirs – a way of warding off the memory of his own displacement?

Still, Poliziano was lucky. Many children without other family resources were left at orphanages, where despite the many caring figures who worked within their walls, the rate of illness and death within the first year of an orphan's arrival was at times as high as 50 per cent. Just as Poliziano uses the word 'exposed' to

---

[9] Poliziano 2000, line 248; p. 159.   [10] Virgil 2006, *Georgics* 4.498, I, pp. 254–5.

[11] Poliziano 2004, pp. 130–1: 'heu durae nimia inclementia legis!' (line 297).

[12] Tissoni-Benvenuti stresses the 'autonomous life' of the theatrical text in the fifteenth century, 'no longer connected to its author, and subject to successive adaptations every time it was newly performed'; Poliziano 2000, pp. 10–11.

[13] Poliziano 2019, p. 22, 'Ad Laurentium medicem'. A letter from 1480 movingly identifies Lorenzo as someone who has offered Poliziano 'not only the protection of a patron, but even the affection of a father'; McGowan 2005, p. 43.

[14] Poliziano 2012, p. viii; Butler 2018, p. 16; Greene 1982, p. 169.

characterize his abandoned play, these children too, many but by no means all infants, were often referred to as *esposti* – or, given the fact that they were found once exposed, *trovatelli* or foundlings. Poliziano was able to bypass this grim future, and the extent to which he did receive care may have made him ever more appreciative of support from friends like Canale, or Lorenzo's cousin, to whom Poliziano again refers to himself as an uncaring parent. In a letter dated 4 November 1482 to Lorenzo di Pierfrancesco de' Medici, Poliziano prefaces the inclusion of his Latin poem *Manto* with the phrase 'You compel me' (cogis tu quidem me). And what Lorenzo has compelled him to do is to publish (*edere*) his unpolished poem, characterized as a deformed or imperfect creature, not unlike the *figliuola* left to languish in the wilds. (The Florentine publisher Antonio Miscomini evidently rushed the work immediately into print before Poliziano could change his mind, given the date on the final page of *Manto*: 6 November.)[15] A poetic rendition of the letter repeats the use of 'to compel': 'It is your chief object of care that my trifles not disappear; and though I am an unwilling parent, you compel them to bear the light of day.'[16] The word *cura* – care – is at the centre of this line, the beginning and end of which are straddled by Poliziano's 'trifles or worthless things': '*Neve meae* permeant *cura* est tua maxima *nugae*' (l. 42). What grounds those worthless words, and presumably gives them worth, is the centring project of Lorenzo's caring, which drives them from the darkness of Poliziano's study into daylight, where they can now belong to others.

Was Poliziano an anomaly? Or were his apparent habits of casting off his works with no concern for their longevity a typical response to the vagaries of the time – or expressions of false modesty? Arguably Ferrante's dismissal of her novels as well as her refusal to reveal her real name and to prolong her association with her works are uncharacteristic of our own era. But was Poliziano's stance vis-à-vis Paul, vis-à-vis himself, equally unusual in the late fifteenth century?

At times Poliziano contradicts himself, particularly when writing about works other than Paul's. He too cared for lost, abandoned, others: if not the apparently mediocre words of the now forgotten Paul, then those of writers worthy of being read. In a dedicatory verse to a compilation of Horace's *Odes* by the Florentine scholar Cristoforo Landino, Poliziano celebrates his contemporary as the one who 'restored you, Horace (te . . . reddidit) to the choruses and the lyre just as you were when you used to play the soothing lute by the waters of Tivoli'.[17] Shrouded for centuries in clouds and covered with dust, Horace is here now (*nunc*) as he used to be; and Poliziano accentuates the 'nowness' of his reappearance by repeating *nunc* three times in the final four lines. And just as Giotto speaks in words Poliziano

---

[15] Poliziano 2004, p. 200.   [16] Poliziano 2019, pp. 128–9.   [17] Poliziano 2019, pp. 310–1.

composed for the painter's cenotaph in the Florentine Duomo ('I am one through whom the extinct act of painting lived again'),[18] so does the Greek historian Herodian speak in Poliziano's translation of his prose into Latin, which allows Herodian to 'travel more broadly and come into the hands of more people'.[19] Thanks to Poliziano, who has rendered – *reddidit* – everything Herodian wrote in Latin words, Herodian can now speak Latin too. If the word Poliziano flung in Paul's face, *edita*, means to give out, *reddere* literally means to give again or to give *back*, as though translation returns something lost to its author.

This seems to be at odds with Poliziano's comments to Canale, Lorenzo di Pierfrancesco de' Medici, and Paul. Surely if Michel Foucault is right, and the author is dead, and surely if Poliziano is right and the poem can no longer be *called* the author's, then there is no need to feel responsibility to the writer.[20] Yet Poliziano's care for others' texts, and his appreciation of those who cared for his own texts, belies the question. Is one's responsibility to the orphaned work, a text that needs future readers rather than a parent? In an oration on the Roman poet Statius, delivered to the Florentine Studio soon after his return from Mantua, Poliziano suggests that we should disregard a writer's thoughts *about* their work and concentrate on the work itself. Even though Statius opens his *Silvae* (modestly) warning that it's not worthy of being read, Poliziano argues that 'we should not pay attention to that which one thinks . . . but to what he has made' (effecerit).[21] The artefact itself – the object, the *thing*, that we hold in our hands, whether a roll, a manuscript, a printed folio – becomes the point of one's commentary. One engages with the work: complete or incomplete, rough or polished, well-raised by a caring parent or cast off by a dismissive one. As Kate van Orden notes, especially with the invention of print, 'Texts cannot escape the uneven world of the objects in which they are captured, exchanged, gifted, commodified, preserved and destroyed' – a process during which, she adds, 'authors lose their sovereignty'.[22]

How to combat this captivity, which is hardly just a result of print? And is Poliziano exhibiting remarkable cruelty or showing us the foresight of an unwithering gaze into the perilous future of any poem: the innocent *figliuola* torn apart by wild beasts. Is he (equally) concerned that he'll suffer the same fate as the less innocent Orpheus if he reveals that he is too attached to his work, and hence, to what he loves? Poliziano's invocation of the *figliuola*, however harsh, implicitly assumes that the author is a caretaker, parent, and guardian who nurtures poetry and sees it through its birth, maturation, and public entrance into the world – a personification that has found numerous forms of expression over at least two millennia, albeit often paired with sentiments of *angst* regarding

[18] Poliziano 2019, p. 171.   [19] Poliziano 2019, p. 169.   [20] Foucault 1979, pp. 141–60.
[21] Poliziano 1952, p. 874.   [22] Van Orden 2013, p. 17.

a work's reception and return. The frequent references to the orphan highlight the necessarily uncertain result of the author's disappearance – and create a space for those who emerge in the author's absence such as scribes, editors, publishers, and translators as a way of acknowledging their own essential work of caring.[23] At the same time, were early modern authors viewed as 'sovereign' in the first place? And to what extent is the eventual creation of that 'sovereignty' dependent on the obfuscation of others' labours – such as those caring readers who, like Canale, bring someone else's work into the world?

Interest in material culture and the history of print over the last several decades has produced a body of scholarship that considers the dynamics of licensing, permissions, and patronage. To an extent we might characterize this scholarship as an ongoing history of the estrangement of an original work from its author, as historians of the book analyse the making of the author's words into what van Orden calls an object – an objectification that tests the reader's liberties as well.[24] Yet we must also question the extent to which the 'author' was already a fixed entity in the early modern world. The interest in paratexts, portraits, and formulas for textual closure has also led to important reflections on attempts to negotiate ownership and interpretation within the shifting contexts of both manuscript and print culture.[25] Additionally, translation studies has enabled exciting new work on the possibilities opened up through the renaissance of both classical and early Christian texts – texts necessarily orphaned throughout the medieval period because of the unavailability of speakers of Greek and scholars of classical Latin.[26]

This is the necessary backdrop for my own interest in ways that early modern readers saw texts as living things that defied objectification – even as they did not automatically regard print as a way of objectifying texts. On the one hand, publishers allowed authors to return to their work during the printing stage as well as afterwards, as they frequently published new, expanded editions and instalments, Tasso, Montaigne, and Milton among them. On the other hand, the non-existence of extended copyright privileges before the eighteenth century meant that authors were far from being perceived as the ultimate 'authorities' over their texts. Just as

---

[23] Other works attending to textual metaphors of orphanhood include Navarrete 1994 and Auerbach 1975, for whom the orphan comes to be 'thought of as a metaphor for the novel itself' as well as for 'the dispossessed, detached self'; p. 395. Sections 2 and 3 will address editors and translators in the production of early modern texts; for the role of the scribe, see Blair 2019.

[24] Chartier 2014, pp. 8–9. On print history: Chartier 1994; Hoffman 1998, Murphy 2000, and Pettegree 2010.

[25] Genette's comment on prefaces is typical of his approach to thinking about the 'objectives' of paratexts: the preface's chief function is '*to ensure that the text is read properly*' (emphasis in the original); p. 197; Sherman 2011 for a reading of what he calls 'terminal paratexts'; on authors' portraits, Bolzoni 2019; on closure, Fowler 1989.

[26] Richardson 2018, Rizzi 2017, Newman and Tylus 2015, Burke 2002, Coldiron 1993.

importantly, with the shift from the fixed Latin language to the vagaries of Europe's fledgling vernaculars, the new kids in town, the early modern period ushers in a new attitude about language itself: fleeting, in motion. Or as Dante says of the dialects spoken in Italy's cities, over a mere fifty-year period one can see 'how many words have been exhausted, and born, and altered' (in qua molti vocabuli essere spenti e nati e variati).[27] This is a process of *trasmutare* or transformation that must be tended to by all who translate and write, conscious of the differences between their tongue and that of their predecessors – and future readers.

The early modern insistence on vernacular languages and texts alike as growing and incomplete results in an entity that not only needed but benefited from others' help. Recourse to metaphors of a family, including the adoptive family, grants wandering works an aura of authenticity and gives them a home, preserving them from the potential depersonalization of the industry – or of any process of transmission that removes something from its source. This is a turn from old families to new ones, for ultimately the return to the author is always a fiction: *né più tua*. But in its place emerges a newfound recognition of the possibilities that distance can confer.[28] Such distance gives the reader the freedom to produce their own interpretations of a text that, as Stephen Orgel has written, is seen as 'alive', evidenced nowhere more than in the marginalia found in manuscripts and printed books alike.[29] Indeed, for Orgel, studies in material culture have enabled us to recover those practices that pre-existed a more modern emphasis on 'pristine books, unmediated by use or even by prior possession' – and hence on the author.[30]

Which is what Poliziano surely recognized. As an editor and translator himself (not unlike Anita Raja, who has been convincingly identified as the 'real' Elena Ferrante), Poliziano was well aware that, without the care of others, many authors' works would be forever forgotten or lost – including his. Indeed, without Canale or Lorenzo di Pierfrancesco, he would have rarely sent anything out. This isn't because he was too lazy to edit his writing or (much more likely) too busy – as he claims to his friend Girolamo Donà, no doubt exaggerating, he has no time for himself, so hassled is he by others' requests for things they want written instead: a motto for the hilt of a sword, 'a line of verse for a bed'.[31] Written in 1490 and thus at the height of his fame, the letter continues: 'as long as I am compelled to belong to everybody, I can never really belong to myself – or to anyone'.[32] *Nec meus esse possum*: I can never be my own. There is only what he has made, and that is for others to take stock of.

---

[27] Dante 1993, Convivio 1.5,9, p. 56.   [28] Stock 1990, pp. 107–9.

[29] Hoffman 1998, p. 101 notes the wide margins of the 1588 edition of Montaigne's popular *Essais*, which 'invited readers to take copious notes' – even as the most 'prolific annotator of his edition' was Montaigne himself (102); see Section 2.

[30] Orgel 2023, p. 25.   [31] Poliziano 2006, p. 127.   [32] Poliziano 2006, p. 128.

These others, in turn, would emerge after his death at barely forty. Had it been up to Poliziano, we wouldn't be reading his epigram to Paul today. During the summer of 1494, Poliziano had been preparing an edition of his Latin poetry for publication (possibly one that included that epigram). He died in September, leaving it unfinished and thus 'unable to send it out' (scito non esse haec edita ab ipso). This is what Aldus Manutius notes in his preface to *Omnia opera Angeli Politiani*, published in 1498.[33] But these are not, despite the title, all of Poliziano's works. Many of Poliziano's papers were lost or dispersed after his death, including that edition of Latin poems, and it was only thanks to his friends ('sed ab amicis') that Aldus has something at all to print. Other pages no doubt lurked in the homes of various Florentines who sought to publish them as their own (ut edant pro suis). Aldus acknowledges that some works in the volume 'lacked finish and refinement', and that Poliziano 'would have made corrections if the opportunity had been granted him' as he continued working to 'shed great light on all the liberal arts' and 'free philosophy from the grasp of the barbarians'.[34] Given Poliziano's concern about the *Orfeo*'s lack of polish, Aldus's claim that the 1498 edition is not what Poliziano would have wished is especially poignant. *Si licuisset*: had Poliziano only been given licence to live and complete the task himself.

The phrase is Ovid's, from his *Tristia*, written after Augustus banished him from Rome in 4 CE. In poem 1.7 he asks a friend to add six lines to the opening of the *Metamorphoses*, the 'work broken off by the unfortunate exile of its master' (infelix domini quod fuga rupit opus).[35] In the next lines, Ovid identifies himself not as *dominus* or lord but as parent. 'All you who touch these rolls bereft of their father, to them at least let a place be granted in your city [i.e., Rome]! ... Whatever defect this rough poem may have he would have corrected, had it been permitted him': 'emendaturus, si licuisset, erat', the final words in the poem, and the line cited by Aldus.

'Had it been permitted': how much licence do authors really have when it comes to how their works circulate in the world? The following pages will chart the drama that emerges as the personified text is released, a drama involving authors themselves as well as those who look after their works in their absence – sometimes having been explicitly entrusted with those words, sometimes not. Moving via the aforementioned Ovid, Horace, and Dante to early modern figures from Erasmus to

---

[33] Manutius 2017, pp. 184–5.
[34] Manutius 2017, p. 187. The *Orfeo* was published a month before Poliziano's death, in Bologna; Canale may have circulated it to printers. It appeared with Poliziano's other major work in Italian, *Stanze per la Giostra*, in honour of Giuliano de' Medici – left unfinished out of grief following Giuliano's assassination.
[35] Ovid 1996, *Tristia* 1.7.35–40, pp. 38–9.

Anne Bradstreet and Sor Juana Inés de la Cruz, the following pages illustrate the dynamics that undermine the fantasy of owning one's words both before and after the revolution of print – dynamics which are arguably exacerbated in our virtual world today. Still, when Jacques Derrida lamented, 'Each time I let something go, each time some trace leaves me, "proceeds" from me, unable to be reappropriated, I live my death in writing',[36] he was reacting not so much to the vagaries of the internet or print but to losing touch with what he felt (wrongly? rightly?) was reduced to 'an artifact that speaks all alone and all alone calls the author by his name, without the author himself needing to do anything else, not even to be alive'.[37] Derrida's comments, from his final interview shortly before his death from cancer in 2004, express what Paul might have thought about the plight of his own words in fifteenth-century Florence, as he tries to interject the author back into words unable to be reappropriated. At the same time, was Poliziano really that different from Paul? Did he, like Ferrante, simply need to let go, violently if necessary, in order to move forward? And where would their words be without the intervention of others whose labours have all too often been marginalized or effaced in the desire to make the author the single, supreme entity behind a text?

As noted, authorial centrality was far from a given in the period under consideration. As the next section will nonetheless lay out, writers since antiquity have often tried to assert a measure of control, however fanciful, over their words. In their efforts we might recognize a set of directives legislating how words should leave their creators and where they should go. How to anticipate and affirm that process of separation but convey it to others? And as the remainder of the Element will then take up, how do those others respond?

1 Lexicons of Goodbyes

> Go, litel book, go litel myn tregedie
>> Geoffrey Chaucer, *Troilus and Criseyde*

> Goe little booke, they self present,
> As child whose parent is unkent . . .
> And when thou art past ieopardee,
> Come tell me, what was sayd of mee:
> And I will send more after thee
>> Edmund Spenser, *Shepheardes Calender*

> Go little book
> and hide
>> Leonard Cohen, *Book of Longing*

---

[36] Taylor 2018, p. 130; from *Learning to Live Finally.*
[37] Taylor 2018, p. 132; from *The Beast and the Sovereign.*

For a book to be read, it must leave its author, an observation seemingly too banal to spend time dissecting. And yet the authors to whom this section turns considered the act of departing from their works anything but banal. They make it edgy, interesting, at times melancholic or tragic. Sometimes the drama occurs at the end of a work, as with Chaucer's *Troilus and Criseyde*, and sometimes at the beginning, as with Spenser's *Shepheardes Calender*. But it's always at a threshold, creating a space both self-consciously removed from the world of literary exchange and all too cognizant of that world beyond. (Leonard Cohen's ironic command that his book leave him – only to hide – is something of an outlier today where send-offs are deemed unnecessary, replaced by a page of acknowledgements or a one-line dedication.) That Chaucer wrote before the era of print and Spenser more than a century after its invention dismisses any possibility that this new technology either inaugurated or silenced a tradition of saying goodbye to one's words.[38] At the same time, print generated new concerns and opportunities alike for those sending off their works, as well as those hesitant to part from them.

Indeed, there is a considerable backstory to these English writers. It involves parchment rolls from first-century BCE Rome, the songs of troubadours, and the *dolce stil novo* or sweet new style. There are many differences between the ways poets in imperial Rome sent off their verses and the habits of their medieval and early modern successors, who for the most part wrote not in Virgil's (or Poliziano's) polished Latin but in the *stil volgare* Poliziano used for his *Orfeo*. But as both Latin and vernacular traditions make clear, the little book has the freedom, perhaps the responsibility, to move and go about, configured now as a freed slave, now as a young girl, now as a widow. The poet, in the meantime, is immobilized, soon to be mute. And while the writers expressing their farewells may not sound as bleak as Jacques Derrida, they are often ambivalent about what they are doing.

But such ambivalence may reside in the fact that what is really silent is the poem. The act of personification 'endows a mute and informed thing with a voice', to quote from the *Rhetorica ad Herennium*,[39] so that the author can imagine, perhaps come to terms with, a work's imminent absence. What kind of protection or instructions does it need as it wanders from its maker?[40] How do the 'humble' forms of the lyric and letter as practised by Horace and Ovid – or lyric poetry in vernacular languages far humbler than Latin – acknowledge the

---

[38] On medieval authorship, see Petrucci 1995 and Minnis 2010. For continuities between medieval and early modern textualities, Chartier 1994.

[39] Lombardi 2018, p. 86; 'cum res muta aut informis fit eloquens', p. 87. Also see Alexander 2007.

[40] On 'the metaphor of text = person' in antiquity, see Zanker 2018, esp. 123–41, focused on texts as children. For medieval examples, see Curtius 1953, pp. 131–4.

fragility of *both* poet and text, while attempting to make amends for what might seem like an abandoned but not unloved child? And – a question raised by Spenser's admonition to his book to 'come back and tell me what was said of me' – does it ever return to its maker? And what happens when it does?

Terms of Separation

Poliziano's taunt to Paul with which we started was not wholly original. It was lurking in the words of the Roman poet Horace, if expressed less caustically and more matter-of-factly, absent an interlocutor. In his *Ars poetica*, Horace lays out rules and advice for would-be writers, including this: anything that you haven't yet circulated or published, you can simply destroy: 'delere licebit/quod non edideris' (note the word Poliziano would use 1,500 years later, *edere*). For, as Horace immediately continues, 'the word once sent forth (missa) can never come back'.[41]

This phrase returns to a Horatian poem that *did* have an interlocutor: not another poet but Horace's own book, the first volume of his *Epistles*. The final letter, in verse like all the rest, provides what Ellen Oliensis has called the 'first full-fledged envoi in the Western tradition',[42] a goodbye that will be seen in countless authors to come, from Chaucer to Spenser – and Leonard Cohen. And yet not all of these authors take the time Horace took to personify his book so carefully. Even fewer present their anthropomorphized texts in similar terms, as a youth or *puer* – and a particular kind of *puer*, a slave 'raised in Horace's household, eager for its freedom, and tempted by the bright lights of the big city'.[43] He is ready, in short, to leave his owner/author. But once this impatient youth has taken off to what can only be an uncertain future given his unreadiness, he cannot come home: 'Off with you, down to where you itch to go. When you are once let out, there will be no coming back' (fuge quo descendere gestis. / non erit emisso reditus tibi).[44] Even if he does find fame, once the bloom of youth has left and he starts to show wear and tear, the used-up, worthless book will realize his mistake, and his author will be proven right. But 'who would care to save an ass against his will?' (1.20.16).

In her magnificent overview, Oliensis introduces Horace's powerful closing poem to his collection as it 'dramatizes the separation of the author from his text, the cutting of the umbilical cord that constitutes this text as a book, an independent creature with its own materiality, its own character, its own destiny' (211). As Horace chafes at his book's longing to leave and display himself

---

[41] Horace 2014, *Ars poetica* 389–90, pp. 482–3.

[42] Oliensis 1995, p. 211. For other Latin and Greek contexts of the envoi, Citroni 1986.

[43] Oliensis 1995, p. 211.   [44] Horace 2014, *Epistles* 1.20.5–6, pp. 388–9.

in public, we witness what Oliensis calls 'a meditation on the conditions of literary survival' (211) and which, in light of the introduction, we might call the fate of the orphaned text. At the same time, Horace seems to have faith that the young *puer* will outlive his older master. He closes his epistle – and the *Epistles* – asking that the boy recite, years from now, a few words about *him*, Horace. Those words sound like an epitaph, listing physical attributes (short, prematurely grey) and social class (born of a freedman father and of slender means) and saying that he completed his forty-fourth year – a reminder, none too subtle, that 'the release of the book prefigures not the apotheosis but the death of the author', as Oliensis points out (222). An inescapable fact emerges from an author who cautioned against premature publication (as in the *Ars poetica*, where he recommends that writers should polish and perfect their works for nine years): unless you send your poems out, they won't be known at all. Or as Horace's Greek predecessor, the Alexandrian poet Theocritus, puts it in the words of a goatherd eager to hear a song from a fellow shepherd during the noonday heat: 'You cannot take your song with you in the end. Hades and forgetfulness are the same.'[45] The real threat is that the song will never leave the insular world that Horace creates for it: that it will literally die.[46]

In contrast to this reluctance – ironized, for sure, given Horace's overwhelming if defensive self-confidence in Epistle I:19, which precedes his farewell to his former slave ('I was the first to plant free footsteps on a virgin soil . . . I was the first to show to Latium the iambics of Paros'; ll. 23–4) – Ovid introduces us to a very different scenario. He wrote some three decades after Horace penned this epistle. Ovid's goodbye comes, moreover, not at the end of his poetic collection the *Tristia* but at the beginning, like Spenser's; and it's ten times as long as Horace's reluctant farewell. In exile in Tomis, in what is now Romania, punished for his titillating *Ars amatoria* as unbefitting the stern moralism of imperial Rome, Ovid directs his opening words to his *liber*.[47] 'Little book, you will go without me – and I envy you not – to the city, whither alas your master is not allowed to go' (Parve – nec invideo – sine me, liber, ibis in urbem, / ei mihi, quo domino non licet ire tuo!).[48] Whereas Horace's reluctance to send his book forth has much to do with his belief, sincere or not, that the book isn't ready,

---

[45] Theocritus 1989, *Idyll* 1.62–3, p. 56. This dynamic of separation is developed more fully in Idyll 16 (see Citroni 1986, p. 116), where Theocritus's poems speak for themselves – unlike Horace's *puer*, who must be spoken *to*. But like the *puer*, they want to leave. As Citroni writes, they 'need external protection: in the poet's empty drawer they find themselves out in the cold, forgotten and uncomfortable' (117).

[46] McCarter 2013, p. 273, concludes that with *Epistles* 1.20 Horace 'gives up such efforts [to control his reception] as futile'.

[47] Williams 2001.   [48] Ovid, *Tristia* 1.1.1–2.

Ovid is anxious to get his words out as soon as he can: 'Vade, sed incultus' (I. 1. 3): go off, even if you're not polished.

The conditions for sending out one's book are not always isolated from historical and personal events, or limited to poetic angst about how good it is; and Horace's poems are not untouched by social conditions of patronage. Still, in opening his *Tristia* with an unambiguous envoi that alludes explicitly to his banishment, Ovid to some extent responds to Horace's playful, privileged posture of a man at ease and half in love with his slave. Ovid's meditation on presence and absence, on the poem's mobility versus the poet's immobility, grounds Horace's self-conscious articulation of the dynamics of poetic production and loss in immediate historical referents. This is not so much as to give the lie to Horace's infatuation with his verses and reluctance to expose them to critique as to insist that other demands can be more pressing. The now-marginalized poet needs to *use* his verses for a tactical purpose, to find a reader who might sympathize with his plight – not least Augustus. This act of separation has a purpose, as the book, diminutive though it may be, is given a job to do in the world. It must dress in a way befitting someone impoverished and in mourning; it mustn't discourage prospective readers. Most importantly, it must find the right reader, someone who sighs 'over my exile, reading your lines with cheeks that are not dry, one who will utter a silent prayer unheard by any ill-wisher, that through the softening of Caesar's anger my punishment may be lightened' (27–30). So does Ovid instrumentalize his distance from the *urbs* as a means of reading the *Tristia*, a distance the poems themselves have bridged, now quite literally in our hands.[49] At the same time, the most poignant expression of that unbridgeability for the poet comes in the stark two lines, 'go in my stead, do you, who are permitted to do so, gaze on Rome! Would that the gods might grant me now to be my book!' (57–8) – a book whose ultimate destination is the poet's home, vacant except for his library.[50] And this is where he expects the papyrus roll that is the *Tristia* to be in conversation with other rolls – one of which, as Alessandro Barchiesi has noted, is the 'orphaned *Metamorphoses*', whose author, as seen earlier, asks a friend to revise it via lines given to the *Tristia* itself.[51]

---

[49] See Newlands 1997 on the relationship with the *Tristia*'s reader. Mordine 2010, p. 531, discusses Ovid's ploy to 'shift the responsibility for the text from the bookroll as the instrument of the author's voice to the reader as the agent who makes the bookroll speak and thus effectively licenses its words'.

[50] While Sobecki is addressing medieval texts, this rings true for Ovid: 'every literary testament, every personal dedication is an attempt by the writer to travel with the text, to be remembered together with their work or perhaps despite it'; Sobecki 2019, p. 5.

[51] Barchiesi 2001, p. 27.

Perhaps the real irony of Ovid's oft-quoted opening is that it *was* a book – his *Ars amatoria*, with its gloating recommendations as to where to go to find lovers in Rome – that got Ovid into trouble. In a strident line from the longest poem in the collection, he writes, 'a book is no index of character' (nec liber indicum est animi; *Tristia* II.357; 80–1). An author, that is to say, *cannot* be his book. Ovid knows it and must hope that Augustus too will separate the author from his words. Hence the sad contrast between the immobilized writer and the book, free to travel as it desires, and therefore free, unlike Ovid, to return home. While Horace effectively banishes his epistles from coming home, in Ovid's case the author himself is banished. Ovid both calls Horace out on his privileged position of otium and deflects Horace's inflated angst about his imperfect work onto his, Ovid's, genuine angst about his imperfect life.

Augustus never responded, and nor did many of Ovid's (so-called) friends. Yet more than a thousand years after Ovid parted from his words in the hope they might bring him back from Tomis, an anonymous glossator would write alongside one of Ovid's verses, 'utilitas tota est lectoris, quia sibi nulla fuit': 'the work's usefulness serves only the reader, it held none for him'.[52] Ovid's verses circulated without him, but they failed to get him what he wanted. The medieval reader's gain is the poet's loss. Yet while Ovid bids his book to seek out the Emperor and 'hand him himself', he tells his *libellus* that its real destination is 'tuam ... domum' (106): your home, where his *fratres* await his arrival – brothers that include the five rolls of the *Metamorphoses*, 'recently saved from the burial of my fortunes' (118). The *Tristia* may not find Augustus, but it will find its family.

What to make of these different itineraries – and how to reflect on their impact in the centuries to come? Chaucer's 'Goe litel booke' and Spenser's 'Go, little booke' owe themselves not to Horace's tense, passive-aggressive address to his freed slave but to Ovid. He sends his papyrus roll off to the uncertain future that Chaucer and Spenser embrace as well, even if Ovid makes its destination a library, a home of familiars far away, while Spenser tells his book to return to his parent. Horace's fixation with the completed work, rubbed with pumice, ending with the author's epitaph, would be echoed in his claim that he made of his *Odes* a 'monument more lasting than bronze' that would enable him to live forever: 'I shall not wholly die.'[53] It suggests an autonomy that could not be Ovid's, at least not after his exile (and Ovid too flirted with self-monumentalization in the *Metamorphoses*). Ovid operates with an entirely different sense of imperatives. He is fixated on getting his work out *now*. The *Tristia*'s professed lack of completion attests not to any artistic fault on the part

---

[52] Keen 2009, p. 149; quoting Hexter 1986, p. 111.   [53] Horace 2004, *Odes* 3.30.1, p. 216.

of the author but to his status as outsider bereft of imperial support, living – as he says at the close – on the edge of the world, seeking to return to the place that Horace never had to leave at all.

Explosion of the *congedo*

'Io mi rivolgo con la faccia del mio sermone a la canzone medesima, e a quella parlo'; '[at the end of the poem], I turn around and address my discourse to the canzone herself, and speak to her'.[54] This is Dante telling us how to end a *canzone*, by way of what is not surprisingly called a *tornada* or *tornata*, since the final stanza should return ('si ritornasse') to the poem itself. The *Convivio*, from which this passage is taken, was itself a way of returning to three *canzoni* that Dante had composed a decade earlier. In addition to providing extensive commentary to his own poems, he also offers reflections on the status of the vernacular, the role of Latin, and – fleetingly, although pointedly – his exile from Florence, already going on four years when he started his ambitious project in 1306 (the *Convivio* was originally slated to have fourteen chapters; he abandoned it after the fourth). Like Ovid, Dante dreamt of returning home. At the same time, unlike Ovid, he was less optimistic about using his writing as the vehicle for that return, even as he asks another canzone not in the *Convivio* to go to Florence, 'my land', to tell it that '[its] maker can no longer make war against you', having now turned his mind to other things.[55] And if Ovid and Horace alike personify their works as young men off to the city, Dante's identifies his canzone in its close as a rustic, uneducated woman from the mountains, 'O montanina mia canzon: tu vai'. Gendered feminine, both the *canzone* and *ballata* were often directed to women, sometimes the love object of the poet, sometimes a prospective patron, sometimes an allegorical figure such as Wisdom. The *tornada* is the place where the poet both returns to the argument of the poem and reflects on its imminent departure to destinations unknown, like Horace's *puer*, or to a 'home' inaccessible to the author himself – like Ovid's slender book.

But if *tornada* connotes return,[56] the word that would come to denote the Occitan tornada in Italy has a somewhat different sense: *congedo*. From the Latin *commeatus*, it signifies the granting of permission in a military sense; eventually it will come to mean a goodbye in and of itself. This is the case with Dante's contemporary Cino da Pistoia (like Dante, from Tuscany) in his ballata 'Angel di Dio', a despairing poem about a young woman resembling an angel

---

[54] Dante 2000, *Convivio* 2.11.1. p. 118.

[55] Petrarch 1979 'Amor, da che convien pur ch'io mi doglia', 76–84, pp. 634–5. Allegretti 2006 notes that Dante, like Ovid, actualizes the distance of the author from his readers – and his text.

[56] Keen 2009 notes that unlike the French *envoi*, which looks outward, the Italian *tornada* has the poet looking 'back at the text', offering a more reflective moment; p. 183.

who has undone him. 'Ballad, if someone asks after your maker, tell them you left him weeping when you went' (Ballata, chi del tuo fattor dimanda, / dilli che tu 'l lassasti / piangendo quando tu t'*acommiatasti*) – literally, when you gave yourself permission to go.[57] The 'fattor' or maker of the *ballata* is in tears, but not because of his song's departure. As we learn in the next terzina, 'you didn't wait to see [the poet] die, since he sends you off (ti manda) so you can digress upon his condition'. The song *does* have her maker's permission to leave just before he dies. It is love that has laid him low, as we know from the rest of the poem, and the finale accentuates both the necessity of the ballata's journey and the definitive separation of the maker from his work. Cino ends telling his poem, 'entrust yourself to every noble heart (A ciascun gentil cor lo raccomanda), since I by myself (per me) am surely unable to procure a means to go on living' (28–30).

Per me, 'by myself'. Alone, the poet can do nothing to ensure that his life will continue – the desperate cry typical of so many a medieval lyric, written about and often to a cruel beloved. But there's another reason for Cino's *ballata* to leave. The *tornata* originally functioned as a directive to the singer of the poet's words. Or as Joan Levin comments, 'The [Occitan] custom of addressing one's song evolved from a long tradition whereby the troubadour entrusted his *canso* to either a *jonglar* or a messenger, who would then transport and/or perform it to a certain lady or to the public.'[58] With the Italian tradition, less dependent on performance, 'the intermediary between a poet and his lady became ... the *canzone* itself'. The poem becomes its own *jonglar*. The act of trust that inhered in the performative mode was between poet and singer, also referred to as a messenger as in Bernart de Ventadorn's 'Messatgers, vai e cor'.[59] With Cino and other Italian poets, the poem itself is now so entrusted. And if the lady refuses to listen, then it is up to the noble hearts of Italy to hear the *ballata*'s words, although the poet does not stipulate what he seeks from them: does he hope they will show him how to go on living, or is his poem looking for shelter in anticipation of his imminent death? What *is* this poem expected to do in the world? And now that the impatient youth of Horace and obedient *libellus* of Ovid have become feminized – their books a slender poem of thirty lines (the length of Cino's *ballata*) – are the author's words more vulnerable as they leave a home to which they cannot return because of what we can only presume to be their *fattor*'s death?

Cino's death, however, was not imminent. He wrote more than 150 poems during his long lifetime, ranging from sonnets and short *ballate* to longer *canzoni*, and one might reasonably ask how seriously to take his investment in – his goodbye to – a single poem such as 'Angel di Dio'. Yet the dynamics of this goodbye move us towards a way of thinking about the poet's relationship to

---

[57] Pirovani 2012, XXIV.22–4, p. 417.   [58] Levin 1984, p. 298.   [59] Ibid.

his words that is very different from what we have seen in Horace and Ovid. Cino's 'lo raccomanda' explicitly conveys a sense of trust in others who will listen: 'ciascun gentil cor', every gentle heart. Over the centuries, *gentile* would take on the nuanced interpretation of someone with good manners, possessed of social grace. But its earliest uses are more explicit about the class differentiation that lies behind the word. If *gentile* does not necessarily mean noble, the 'gentle reader' is superior insofar as they are more likely than others to be responsive to another's words.

In order to attract such a reader, Dante offers additional comments on poetic closure towards his own close of the unfinished *Convisio*. 'At the end of his work, every good craftsman should render it as noble and as beautiful as he can, so that it depart from him ever more distinguished and of worth' ('ciascuno buono fabricatore, ne la fine del suo lavoro, quello nobilitare e abbellire dee in quanto puote, acciò che più celebre e più prezioso da lui si parta'; IV.xxx).[60] These are sound rhetorical principles that go back to Cicero, Seneca, and others, who urged that an orator should always end with what is strongest. But what is new is Dante's neologism, *nobilitare*, or to render noble. And it's particularly striking given that he's using it with reference to a mere craftsman or *fabrica-tore*, someone skilled in the lowly language of Italian rather than the (already) noble language of Latin. Dante's neologism is connected to the edgy word 'abbellire', to make (more) beautiful by adding an ornament or, in this instance, adorning the poem. The poem's *tornata* becomes such an act of adornment, 'added on' as an entirely new and separate strophe, often differentiated from the rest of the poem because of its metre or, more frequently, number of lines. But it can only be truly 'en-nobled' by virtue of its listener, such as 'la donna nostra' to whom the canzone on which Dante is commenting at the close of the *Convivio* is directed.[61] Its true *adornmento* is the reader who will grant it the dignity and nobility that it otherwise lacks, simply by acknowledging that the poem is worthy of being read.

The 'noble' *tornata* thus turns not only back to the poem but outward towards a 'noble' listener.[62] 'You'll go out, canzone, since I won't hide you from anyone who desires you',[63] writes Antonio da Tempo at the end of

---

[60] Dante 1999, p. 337.

[61] Dante 1999, 'Li Dolci Rime', 141–6, p. 220. When the canzone arrives before the lady, she should tell her, 'I go speaking of your friend (*l'amica vostra*)' – an 'amica' who is *gentilezza* itself; 146.

[62] The *tornata* also stages what Agamben 1999 called the 'catastrophe and loss of identity' at the ending of the medieval poem; p. 12. See Watkin 2010, p. 135, for further thoughts: 'the poem must die through a process of self-alienation to become what it is destined to be'.

[63] 'Tu andarai, canzon, ch'i non t'ascondo / in vista di zascun che n'avrà voglia!'; Keen 2009, p. 185.

a canzone (the reverse of Leonard Cohen), while a *ballata* attributed to Dante is told to go to 'that lovely woman without delay' (movi, ballata, senza gir tardando / a quella bella donna).[64] The conviction that the poem will find the 'cor gentil' to whom it can entrust itself is strikingly different from Horace's trepidation about his *puer*'s premature exit, or Ovid's slender hope that his exile can be arrested. Dante is confident that his messenger – configured as a physical, bodily entity that moves, takes up space, occupies a place in the world as it talks and sings, as Elena Lombardi observes – will find solace in the company of another caretaker.[65]

Or another poem. Like Ovid's *Tristia*, which heads towards the author's library in Rome, the *ballata* frequently has a family beyond its maker. After Beatrice dies in *Vita Nova*, Dante tells his canzone 'Li occhi dolenti' to 'go out weeping, and find again the women and young ladies to whom your sisters (le tue sorelle) were once accustomed to bringing happy news'. Dante's allusion to what Lombardi calls 'sister songs' 'creat[es] a veritable sisterhood of women readers and female songs' – even as those sisters carried a very different message from the news that 'Li occhi dolenti' conveys with her words of grief.[66]

The short *ballata* and longer *canzone* might have seemed ephemeral presences on the literary map, and Dante no doubt composed his *Vita Nova* and *Convivio* precisely to give poems that once circulated separately a textual 'family'. But while the young woman may be assumed to be needier than Horace's apparently defenceless *puer*, she isn't helpless. Even without such larger contexts, the individual poem does not presume to manage alone, or leave without its maker's blessing. Perhaps precisely because of its female gender, and because it speaks in its mother tongue, it recognizes that it needs others. This adornment provided by another ballata or the right reader creates a very different model from what we saw in the classical texts, even as the library of Ovid's books arguably looks to this future chorus. Yet even Dante, perhaps the most complex of medieval poets, knows how tenuous an author's hopes of being understood really are. Thus the tentative close of the canzone 'Tre donne': 'But *if* it should ever happen that you find someone who is virtue's friend ... then show yourself to him.'[67]

---

[64] Dante 1995, 'In abito di saggia messaggiera', 2–3; p. 253.

[65] Lombardi 2018, p. 78. Lombardi adds that the poem licensed to leave by its maker 'opens itself up to the plurality of interpretation' – an act of engagement that 'takes the form both of the protection and clothing of the naked truth, and even of a precious accessory to it' (81).

[66] Lombardi 2018, p. 99. While Lombardi opens her chapter 'Women as Text, Text as Woman', stressing the male coterie readers of Dante's and others' poems, she ends discussing women readers' role in constructing textual identity. See also Barolini 2006, pp. 350–1, on the *congedo*'s creation of women as subjects and interlocutors in Dante's 'Doglia mi reca'.

[67] Dante 1995, 'Tre donne', p. 179: 'Ma s'elli avvien che tu alcun mai truovi / amico di virtú ... / poi li ti mostra', 96–9.

This is why there is strength in numbers. This is the family that looks ahead to Spenser's hope to 'send more after thee': younger brothers and sisters, after the oldest child returns to his father. But neither Spenser nor Ovid alludes to mothers. Dante and his Catholic compatriots saw things differently. A decade after abandoning his *Convivio*, Dante closes his *Commedia* by invoking the noblest mother of all, Mary. Not accidentally, the verb *nobilitare*, coined by Dante at the abrupt close of *Convivio*, returns for the second and last time in *Paradiso*'s final canto. In what could be considered his *congedo* to the entire *Commedia* – suggestively called by Teodolinda Barolini a collection of 'one hundred *canzoni* stitched together'[68] – Dante addresses the gentlest heart imaginable in words uttered not by the *fabricatore* of the poem but by St Bernard of Clairvaux, who addresses Mary as 'you who so ennobled human nature (*nobilitasti sí*) that its Creator did not disdain his being made its created'.[69] By bringing back the word used in the *Convivio* to advise poets, Horace-like, how to strengthen their work, Dante suggests that Mary herself dignifies human nature and, in turn, his poem. The lowly handmaiden who bore the divine being who created her, Mary becomes a paradigm for the miracle Dante seeks for the *Commedia*, written in the vulgar, mother tongue of Dante's Florentine dialect.

Dante wasn't the only poet to seek out Mary, as is clear from the ending of a work that is more a Horatian and Ovidian collection than epic narrative on the order of Dante's *Commedia*: Petrarch's *canzoniere*. Or as he calls it in Latin, the 'rerum vulgarium fragmenta', 366 fragments written in the vulgar tongue, one for each day of the year. Like Horace, Petrarch was notoriously reticent about sharing his work with others; he kept under lock and key his manuscripts of his letters as well as that of the *Canzoniere*, on which he worked for some four decades.[70] The collection is notable for its many moving *congedi* to its canzoni – including several that depart from the enthusiastic send-offs of Dante or Cino. The first poem written after the beloved Laura's death, 268, depicts the canzone wearing the black robes of a widow and proscribes her from going anywhere other than to be with those who similarly mourn – the new family for Petrarch's poems in times of plague. Two earlier canzoni, 125 and 126, are instructed to linger with their author, an implicit return to Horace's emphasis on polishing verses before letting

---

[68] Barolini 2006, p. 45.

[69] Dante, 1984, *Paradiso* 33:4–6: 'tu sei colei che l'umana natura / nobilitasti sí, ch'il suo fattore / non disdegnò di farsi sua fattura'. That the early lyrics to women were based on *laude* or praise poems of the Madonna is clear from Guido Guinizelli's poems to what Barolini 2006 calls a 'theologically ennobled lady'; p. 32.

[70] On Petrarch's fixation with the 'author's book' and desire for 'perfect textuality, directly emanating from the author and warranted by his autograph', see Petrucci 1995, p. 194; Billanovich 1947, pp. 297–302.

them out. Thus Canzone 125 is described as a *poverella* or 'poor little song' and told to 'stay here in these woods' – 'rimanti in questi boschi' – with its uncultivated author and without a reader's conferral of *dignità*.[71]

But someone else can confer that dignity. As expressed in his penultimate letter to his contemporary Boccaccio, Petrarch too believed in endings characterized by strength and persuasiveness. While he would not use the Dantesque neologism *nobilitare* – he was writing to Boccaccio in Latin – he invokes the term *validiora*: books must close with what is strongest.[72] If Boccaccio is Petrarch's last interlocutor in his epistolary collections, the 'Vergine bella' is Petrarch's final interlocutor in Italian. He speaks with her directly, rather than depending on a saint.[73] After praising Mary for twelve stanzas, he arrives at the end of the poem, and thus of the *Canzoniere* itself:

> Il dì s'appressa, et non pote esser lunge,
> sí corre il tempo et vola,
> Vergine unica et sola,
> e 'l cor or conscientia or morte punge.
> Raccomandami al tuo Figliuol, verace
> homo et verace Dio,
> ch'accolga 'l mio spirto ultimo in pace.

(The day draws near and cannot be far, time so runs and flies, single sole Virgin; and now conscience, now death pierces my heart: commend me to your Son, true man and true God, that He may receive my last breath in peace.)[74]

So does Petrarch adorn his overwhelmingly secular *canzoniere* with a religious *congedo*, addressing the only reader who might 'en-noble' the poem's creator as well as his poems. Even if Luca Marcozzi suggests that Petrarch's once open text is now closed, this conferral to the mother who strengthens all serves to introduce it into a new family, which includes Mary's son.[75] Mary also becomes the writer's advocate for his vernacular poems in which he claims to have captured his life: and from whom he asks approval for what Paolo Cherchi calls this 'canto "umanistico" alla *dignitas hominis*'[76] – a humanistic song to human dignity.

Yet while Mary is undeniably unique ('sola al mondo senza esempio', 366:53), she also models those readers whom Petrarch hopes, perhaps trusts, will engage with his writings and pass them on to another 'cor gentil'. While the final canzone claims that this has all been for the eyes of Mary and Christ

---

[71] Petrarch 1979, *Rime* 125: 79–81, pp. 243–4. See Levin 1984 on the two *tornadas* of 125 and 126 as a single *congedo*; p. 306.

[72] Petrarch 2017, *Seniles* 17:3:10, Vol. 4, p. 446.

[73] On Petrarch's indebtedness to the final canto of the *Commedia*, see Martinez 2009, pp. 348–50.

[74] Petrarch 1979, *Rime* 366: 131–7, pp. 582–3.   [75] Marcozzi 2015, p. 59.

[76] Cherchi 2008, p. 173.

alone, this fiction was undermined at the start by Petrarch's proemial sonnet to earthly readers, the 'Voi' who hear his scattered rhymes.[77]

This deliberate care for the work finds its antithesis in one of the first women to have her works published in Italy: the widowed aristocrat Vittoria Colonna, whose 'carelessness' about who read her poems might be gleaned in her indifference to publication, even as thirteen editions of her poems appeared in her lifetime.[78] But she did care about one particular reader (although not Mary). In the penultimate sonnet of a gift manuscript for Michelangelo, compiled in the early 1540s, Colonna disowns the Horatian preoccupation with polishing as she calls attention to her failure 'to take up the file (la lima) of good sense' and her refusal to 'embellish or erase [her] rough, uncultivated verses'.[79] This is a direct retort to the author of the *Ars poetica*. But this is because Colonna seeks neither praise for herself nor – her eye always on her own death – to have her verses live on in the world after what she confidently predicts will be her 'joyful return to heaven'; l. 7). Instead, she links the spontaneity of her writing to the divine fire that 'inflames [her] mind' – a fire from which 'sparks issue forth of their own accord' (escan fore / Mal mio grado talor queste faville; ll. 10–11). The final terzina revises Horace's angst over letting one's words out too soon: 'if one such spark should once warm / some gentle heart, then a thousand times / a thousand thanks I owe to that happy mistake' (Et s'alcuna di lor un gentil core / Avien che scaldi, mille volte e mille / Ringraziar debbo il mio felice errore) – the mistake, presumably, of failing to polish her verses before letting them go. It is worse to bury one's candle under a bushel than to send forth a single imperfect flame.[80]

Colonna gives no directive as to where this poem, or its 102 sisters (or given that they are all sonnets, *fratelli*) should go. Colonna is not Ovid; she is comfortably living on the island of Ischia, not on the Black Sea, and needs no 'cor gentil' to authorize her verse. Her manuscript for Michelangelo seems to have been a gift freely given without expectations of anything in return.[81] Perhaps this is why her final sonnet in the Michelangelo manuscript is not an orchestrated farewell to the collection but a rejection of further poetry. If her penultimate sonnet embraces the flame as a stimulus to writing, her final sonnet asks that fire to 'embrace and burn [her] heart in silence', ensuring that she write no more. Petrarch asks Mary and, through Mary, Jesus to read his poems. Colonna asks that the one who 'listens from heaven' – God himself – read

---

[77] *Rime* 1, 'Voi ch'ascoltate in rime sparse', 'You who hear in scattered rhymes'; Petrarch 1979, pp. 36–7.

[78] Crivelli 2016.

[79] Colonna 2005, 'S'in man prender non soglio unqua la lima', 102:1–4, pp. 136–7.

[80] See Prodan 2014 for a discussion of Sonnet 102; pp. 138–9.

[81] On the dynamics of the gift in Colonna and Michelangelo, see Nagel 1997.

nothing, only that he hear her voice 'interrupted by grief and by hoarse cries: that's what the song should be like for him who listens from heaven, who attends to our heart and not our style' (Interrotto dal duol, dal pianger roco / Esser dee il canto vèr colui ch'ascolta / Dal cielo, e al cor non a lo stil riguarda [103, ll. 12–4]). Colonna's close to her manuscript for Michelangelo is neither a goodbye nor a reflective return to the argument of her verses. It is not an attempt to make those poems stronger, except in directing itself to a God who goes unnamed (colui), and who cares not for how she puts her words together. Nor does he care for those words themselves. All that matters are the sounds of her grief for having presumably made so little of her life, for having devoted so much time to writing.

While Colonna's poems were printed by others as early as 1538 – several years prior to her Michelangelo manuscript – she never produced her own authorized edition. The impetuous editor of the 1538 volume, one Philippo Pirogallo, had hoped for just that: once Colonna could see his admittedly imperfect version of some 145 poems, ideally she would be moved to send them out into the light of day herself, correcting his own transcriptions.[82] But Colonna did no such thing. Her refusal to be involved in her own publications – or to weigh in on the efforts of others – suggests for Abigail Brundin 'the level of propriety and humility required by the aristocratic woman writer, who cannot admit to a desire for acclaim or publicity and less still for monetary gain'.[83] While this may be the case, her nonchalance about sharing works entrusted to her by friends suggests that she was not one to readily defend an author's proprietary rights. This doesn't mean that her friends agreed. Baldassare Castiglione, about whom we'll hear more in Section 2, angrily addresses Colonna's (mis)treatment of his manuscript of the *Courtier*: 'Now being in Spain, and being informed from Italy that signora Vittoria della Colonna . . . to whom I had already given a copy of the book, had, contrary to her promise, caused a large part of it to be transcribed, I could not but feel a certain annoyance, fearing the considerable mischief that can arise in such cases.'[84] For someone who believed in the arbitrary path a spark might take long after she has pledged to write no more, it's no surprise that Colonna encouraged such chance encounters, disseminating the words of her friends. As anti-Horatian as Colonna might seem given her disdain for polishing and perfecting her writing, there was one point on which she and Horace would have agreed. One's words never come home; the spark or *scintilla* can only be felt by others, who will take

---

[82] Colonna 2021, pp. 34–5: 'she will be able to see them again, and send them into the light of day' (mandargli in luce).
[83] Colonna 2005, p. 18.   [84] Castiglione 1959, p. 1.

those words elsewhere – prompting an anxious Castiglione to rush to the press with his latest, definitive version of what would soon become one of Europe's most popular texts.

When Poems Stay Put

The young Spenser did request to see his poem again. This was at the beginning of a career that would span almost two decades, culminating in his *Faerie Queene*, dedicated to Elizabeth I. His *Shepheardes Calender* of 1579 is a salvo, sent off to another well-known political figure, Sir Philip Sidney. To represent that beginning, the genre in which Spenser chose to cast his fledgling efforts was the one that Virgil chose, the pastoral. While the *Calender* ranges across a wide array of literary stances and comes complete with the pedantic commentary of one mysterious E. K. – a presumably trusted reader of 'gentil core' who evidently read and approved the project – it is a collection of twelve eclogues so as to match the months of the year, expanding Virgil's ten. Spenser's *congedo*, placed at the beginning of the *Calender*, is not a *congedo* from a life or literary career. It is a launching *of* that career, as the young poet awaits one book's return and prepares to send out another.

If the unkent Spenser waits at home, other authors occasionally walk away from their work. This was Jacopo Sannazaro, whose *Arcadia*, like Colonna's poems, was rushed into print by others anxious to get out a text they felt had been left in someone else's drawer for too long. Unlike Colonna, Sannazaro fought back (helped by friends). A major figure in Neapolitan cultural life in the late fifteenth century, Sannazaro joined the Aragonese King Federico IV in exile in France for several years. During that time, an incomplete manuscript version of his *Arcadia*, a mix of short prose chapters and pastoral eclogues sung by shepherds in a land visited by the disconsolate Neapolitan Sincero (a not-so-veiled cover for the poet himself), was published in Venice. While the unauthorized version consisted of ten chapters, a concerned friend proceeded to publish, probably at Sannazaro's urging, what was billed as the authoritative, correct version of *Arcadia*, now with twelve chapters and a prose *congedo* called 'A la sampogna': to his bagpipe.

This is not a *congedo* à la Spenser, or Horace – or, despite Sannazaro's voluntary exile, Ovid.[85] In a few brief pages, the author reverses the normal pattern of earlier goodbyes. *He* goes off, while the book stays behind, personified as the bagpipe or pastoral instrument *par excellence*. Returning, as it were, to Petrarch's request that his 'poverella' stay in the woods, Sannazaro admonishes his *sampogna*, 'content yourself with your rusticity [and] remain among these solitudes' ('ti admonisco,

---

[85] Ovid is relevant, since, as Carlo Vecce notes, Sannazaro most likely wrote the *congedo* after his departure for France; Sannazaro 2013, pp. 38–40.

che de la tua selvatichezza contentandoti tra queste solitudini ti rimanghi').[86] To this extent, the author's exit from Arcadia mimics that of his character, who in the final chapter of the expanded work returns to Naples, where he has become unrecognizable, so transformed was he by his sojourn. But the closing words to the *sampogna* make it clear that this rustic instrument on which Sannazaro sang remains in place, perhaps to be found by another melancholic lover who will wander into Arcadia and be inspired to sing his own version.

That is the opposite of what had happened to Sannazaro's manuscript, thrust out of Arcadia and into the public eye by a Venetian printer before it was complete. Sannazaro cleverly rewrites its fate – or attempts to rewrite it, well knowing that this mournful instrument has already had its songs materialized as text, its complicated metrical lines organized as words on a printed page before the author was ready to part with it. At the same time, the fiction that Sannazaro perpetrates through his *congedo* as he joins Horace, Ovid, Cino, and Dante trades the poem's mobility for the author's. It may simply be his own way of returning not to the prototypical exile Ovid but to the perfectionist Horace: poem, stay home. But you won't find me there anymore. Leaving the pastoral world behind along with the Italian vernacular, Sannazaro went on to write a Latin epic based on the noble mother Mary, just as the once-unknown Spenser would go on to compose an English epic for his queen. In both cases, the texts unequivocally belong to their readers, in what both Spenser and Sannazaro along with the authors discussed in this section stage as a potentially intimate handoff – at times in the company of a family of sisters and brothers. In the meantime, the intense nature of so many poetic goodbyes reminds us that the struggle to let go is real.

2 Speaking for/to the Dead

I only wish it had been permitted for me to do [this] when . . . Pontano himself was [still] alive . . . He would have seen with what care (curae), effort, and toil we had put into type his most learned and divine poems. He would have seen that the results of his own labours, as well as his short poems, his offspring (pignora), so to speak, were loved, embraced and honoured by both students and men of great learning. I am sorry then that this did not happen and even now I feel it most grievously.[87]

When I was singing of gods and the dreadful arms of the Cyclopes . . . the savage goddesses cut the thread of my life. . . This is why we ourselves did not publish (edidimus) [our verses]. My family out of duty (pia cura) has supplied my poetry, such as it is, alongside my father's. If it had been permitted me, I would have corrected whatever faults our unpolished verses have.[88]

---

[86] Sannazaro 2013, p. 325; Sannazaro 1966, p. 151.   [87] Manutius 2017, pp. 210–11.
[88] Manutius 2017, pp. 222–3.

From the dedicatory pages of two books published in Venice in the early sixteenth century, we have two expressions of deep regret over sudden deaths that deprived authors of seeing their publications. The first one introduces the Latin works of Giovanni Pontano, a friend and colleague of Sannazaro, which appeared in the spring of 1505, two years after the author's death. The other represents verses 'spoken' by the author himself, the young Ercole Strozzi, who died at the age of thirty-six. Like his father, whose poems are published in the same volume, he was a leading cultural figure in the city of Ferrara.

Both of these dedications are from the press of the most innovative and successful printer in Italy, if not Europe: the aforementioned Aldus Manutius, who began printing classical works in Latin and Greek in the late 1490s.[89] While many of Manutius's texts were centuries if not millennia old, in these two cases – as in that of Poliziano, seen earlier – the authors were of recent memory. Pontano perished while his works were in press, and Manutius is chastened by his inability to allow Pontano to see the finished text: had he only been more hasty, had certain messengers who were bringing him Pontano's manuscripts not died en route! For Strozzi's text, published in 1513, Aldus imagines the recently departed young man, once his student, deprived of sending out his book ('non ipsi edidimus'). In both instances, the role of family is stressed. Pontano's offspring, his verses, is cared for by a new family that consists of men of learning; Strozzi's biological family, moved by *pia cura* or compassionate care, gave their brother's and father's words to Aldus. Aldus closes the ten-line verse echoing an earlier dedication for Poliziano: 'If it had been permitted me, I would have corrected whatever faults our unpolished verses have' – the line from Ovid's *Tristia*.[90] Ovid references his exile; Aldus references the premature deaths of Poliziano and Strozzi alike, warning readers that they may encounter moments less than perfect in what follows (and implying that those faults are not his). Taking care of the dead, imagining their wishes for their offspring in the hopes of founding new families: this is Aldus's intention as he created for himself a substantial niche role in the relatively new business of publishing, invoking Strozzi's family and their *pia cura* as a model for his own.

The *congedo* is premised on an act of quasi-simultaneity, the fiction that the poem has just left its author and is now before the reader. But what happens when there is no *congedo* – when the author has been deprived of the chance to say goodbye and their work falls to others? We are back to the language of what becomes, in the aftermath of trauma, a truly orphaned text, as the *gentil core*

---

[89] For background, see Lowry 1979, who emphasizes the uneven quality of some of Aldus's editions.

[90] Manutius 2017, pp. 186–7: 'he would have made corrections if the opportunity had been granted him'.

becomes the editor, inserting himself or herself into the role of the messenger who sends things out (*edere*). Such is Aldus's intervention, one that requires a different kind of mediation. Wandering texts discovered by gentle readers: to a large extent, humanism as practiced by Aldus and many of his contemporaries was an extension of the principles of the canzone that sought to define for herself a readership she could trust, providing adornment and more. If the author sought to create a family for their words consisting of sisters, brothers, and a *cor gentil*, this is now the work of editors as well as translators. The pages that follow consider translation in its broad and narrow senses, as texts without their authors are guided across gaps at once linguistic and chronological so they can be sent out – possibly for the first time, unquestionably in formats very different from their 'original' or intended ones.

This is by no means a straightforward process. This is evident from a quite literal scene of a dying author consigning his works to a future editor. In August 1563, the then thirty-year-old Michel de Montaigne wrote his father a lengthy letter concerning the last few days of his dear friend, Etienne de La Boétie. Montaigne spent those days by La Boétie's bedside, where his friend gave him his library and papers, explicit acknowledgments of Montaigne's affection for *lettres* as well as La Boétie's affection for Montaigne.[91] Montaigne gladly complies, but La Boétie becomes increasingly agitated in his final hours, asking that Montaigne 'de luy donner une place': give him a place. As Montaigne writes: 'Even when I had remonstrated with him very gently that he was letting the illness carry him away . . . he repeated even more strongly: "my brother, my brother, do you then refuse me a place?"' (Mon frere, mon frere, me refusez-vous doncques une place?).[92] Montaigne reassures him that he does still have a place (son lieu), given that he continues to speak. It is not, however, the right place, or as La Boétie puts it, 'not the one I need'. That place is assuredly in heaven, Montaigne piously responds, where La Boétie says that he has been trying to go to 'for the last three days'. An hour later, he gives up the ghost.

But the question haunts Montaigne. As La Boétie's literary executor, for the next seven years he sought to give La Boétie a place as he published the works left to him after his friend's sudden death, including his translations of Xenophon's *Oeconomicus* and Plutarch's *Rules of Marriage* and an edition of some of La Boétie's sonnets in French.[93] Additional sonnets, discovered

---

[91] Montaigne 1967, p. 1050; Montaigne 1962, Vol. II, p. 591.

[92] Montaigne 1967, p. 1055; Montaigne 1962, Vol. II, p. 599.

[93] He tells Michel de L'Hôpital that he seeks to 'place [La Boétie] in the public eye' ('m'a il prins envie de le mettre au jour') by publishing his Latin poems; Montaigne 1967, p. 1059; Montaigne 1962, Vol. II, p. 604.

sometime later by a friend, were given a place in Montaigne's own *Essais*, constituting the twenty-ninth essay of Book 1. At the end of 1.28, where he introduces his friend's poems, Montaigne begs any readers who might have other 'bits and pieces' of La Boétie's writings to send them to him, so he might publish them too.[94] But oddly, the last version of the *Essais* published in Montaigne's lifetime, in 1588, replaces the poems with a terse note alluding to the sonnets' appearance elsewhere: 'Ces vers se voient ailleurs.'[95] La Boétie's place in the *Essais*, that formidable tome that grew ever larger with each edition, is quietly negated.[96]

This, however, is not the only work by La Boétie 'missing' in the *Essais*. They should have also been the place for a work that Montaigne himself discovered in the library left to him by La Boétie: 'Un discours de LA SERVITUDE VOLONTAIRE, et qualches memoires de nos troubles sur l'edict de Janvier 1562.' A passionate treatise against tyranny, the *Discours* is 'a celebrated and creatively original call for civil disobedience' according to one recent account.[97] In the dedicatory letter to his 1571 edition of La Boétie's translations where Montaigne mentions his 'discovery', Montaigne explicitly states as to why he wasn't publishing the *Discours* immediately: it is 'too delicate' ('trop delicate') to be left 'abandon[ed]' 'to the gross and heavy air of so unpleasant a season' ('au grossier et pesant air d'une si mal plaisante saison').[98] And perhaps understandably so. This deeply anti-monarchical work could easily be construed as protesting the French crown's defiance of Protestant tendencies in the early years of the Reformation; the attack on the Huguenots, the St Bartholomew's Day Massacre, would occur in August 1572. But when the *Essais* appeared almost a decade later, Montaigne could not bring himself to put it there either. In the essay where he speaks most directly about La Boétie – his essay on friendship, 'De l'amitié' – he references another discovery. He heard that the *Discours* 'had once been published to an evil end by those who seek to disturb and change the state of our national polity without worrying whether they will make it better... [and so] I have gone back on my decision to place it here' – 'le loger icy'.[99] Respectful of the 'author's reputation', he opines that this was a subject 'treated by [La Boétie] in his childhood purely as an exercise'.

---

[94] These sonnets were found by chance by 'le sieur de Poiferré', then sent to Montaigne. Montaigne goes on to request that anyone who comes upon 'plusieurs lopins de ses escris, par cy, par là' send them his way (Montaigne 1962, Vol. I, p. 212). The sonnets were indeed published elsewhere; see Defaux 2001, and Pozen 2003.

[95] Montaigne 1962, Vol. II, p. 213.   [96] For more elaboration, see Tylus 2023.

[97] La Boétie and Bonnefon 2007, p. 9.

[98] Montaigne 1962, Vol. II, p. 606; Montaigne 1967, p. 1061.

[99] Montaigne 1962, Vol. I, p. 211; Montaigne 1967, p. 200.

Verdict: even the best of friends may choose not to observe to the letter a dear friend's dying request – or let other factors intervene to prevent it.[100] Montaigne moves from giving La Boétie a significant place in his *Essais* to effacing that place; or never providing it at all. And in the meantime, the now empty pages are filled with his incessant, seemingly unending, labours of writing – effectively replacing La Boétie with himself, or, more precisely, La Boétie's work with his own.

Where does the author end, the editor begin? This is a question the Roman poet Martial, some hundred years after Horace's ode to his *libellus*, stages via his *Epigrams*, as he asks his friend Severus to 'read and criticize [his] trifles'. Thanks to Severus's editing, 'this little book' will feel safe (*secures*) and will ultimately owe him 'much more than its master' (*dominus*).[101] In Martial's case, however, the master was very much still alive when his friend critiqued his trifles. As compassionate editor of the work of a friend now gone, Montaigne stages his drama for us in a particularly ingenious way. He is also acting as a kind of censor. His insistence that the *Discours* has already been published by 'vile authors' and used for disturbing ends results in his refusal to bring to light what La Boétie's actual intentions may have been. And yet, it is also the case that Martial closes his short, thirteen-line epigram with a reference to the 'censorial file' (censorial ... lima) of another reader, Secundus. One of the jobs of an editor, as Martial suggests – and perhaps implicitly, Montaigne as well – is to cut: to leave (some) words behind.

Yet one path Montaigne could have taken would have been to have rescued the *Discours* for other readers, to make it right. Aldus frequently claims to do just this, as he corrects texts hijacked from their original authors and intents. Such is apparent in one of his first editions of an ancient Latin author, Julius Maternus, who is now 'return[ed] to Italy all the way from Greece, complete and unimpaired, and looks again upon his kinsmen and his native land. For the edition that has been in wide circulation (*vagabatur* – literally, wandering) before this one is dreadfully corrupt and fragmentary (mutilus) as well as lacking almost half of the work.'[102] This could have become Montaigne's responsibility vis-à-vis his friend: an act of making whole, via his own act of piety or *pia cura*.[103]

It was not merely humanists like Aldus who devoted themselves to such work. Perhaps one of the most famous references to the textual offspring of a deceased author is the dedicatory page of Shakespeare's First Folio, by friends as close to the bard as Montaigne was to La Boétie. Or as John Heminge and

---

[100] Perhaps the most famous example is Virgil's request of his friend Varius that his unfinished *Aeneid* be burnt; Donatus 2008, par. 39.

[101] Martial 1993, 5.80; I, pp. 390–1. The earlier Loeb edition translated 'dominus' as 'author'; Martial 1968; I, pp. 352–3. My thanks to one of the anonymous readers for suggesting the relevance of Martial for this Element.

[102] Manutius 2017, p. 4.   [103] On *cura*, see Hamilton 2013; Zak 2010.

Henry Condell write: 'We have but collected them, and done an office to the dead, to procure his Orphanes, Guardians; without ambition either of selfe-profit, or fame: onely to keepe the memory of so worthy a Friend, & Fellow alive, as was our S H A K E S P E A R E, by humble offer of his playes' – an offering to William, Earl of Pembroke and Philip, Earl of Montgomery.[104] Shakespeare's plays had become orphans, 'out-living him, and he not having the fate, common with some, to be exequutor to his owne writings'.[105] But two well-appointed men who apparently enjoyed seeing the plays onstage can now guarantee their safety, as the writers insinuate when they observe: 'There is a great difference, whether any Booke choose his Patrones, or finde them: This hath done both. For, so much were your L.L. likings of the severall parts, when they were acted, as before they were published, the Volume ask'd to be yours' (A2 v). In this apparent shift from author to works, Heminge and Condell claim to effect the book's wishes – responding to and speaking *for* the text, presumed to be identical to the plays which the Patrones enjoyed onstage.

And yet, they hasten to add, Shakespeare would have done the same, had he only lived. To contextualize the phrase just cited: 'we hope, that (they out-living him, and he not having the fate, common with some, to be exequutor to his owne writings) you will use the like indulgence toward them, you have done unto their parent' (A2–A2 v). In Shakespeare's absence, the 'Friends' perform what they call 'an office to the dead' – providing for his survivors. That provision includes a special kind of care for the survivor's body. Whereas editions of single plays proliferated throughout Shakespeare's lifetime and afterwards, the First Folio is poised to take back what are characterized as unauthorized thefts of Shakespeare's work – a job that falls not only to the two guardians of the Folio but to the 'great Variety of Readers' whom Heminge and Condell implore to *buy* Shakespeare's work ('The fate of all bookes depends . . . not of your heads alone, but of your purses . . . buy it first . . . whatever you do, Buy'; A3). And readers should buy *their* book because this version of Shakespeare's works is far superior to the scattered editions of individual plays already in print. 'Where (before) you were abused with diverse stolne, and surreptitious copies, maimed, and deformed by the frauds and stealthes of injurious impostors, that expos'd them : even those, are now offer'd to your view cur'd, and perfect of their limbes; and all the rest, absolute in their numbers as he conceived them' (A3).

This echoes Poliziano's tormented language about the *Orfeo*. Yet Shakespeare's plays were 'maimed' and 'deformed' not because they needed polishing but because 'injurious impostors' misrepresented them. Perhaps Shakespeare's care-lessness or lack of caring led to such mutilation by others, as the friends of

---

[104] Shakespeare 1623, A2v.   [105] Shakespeare 1623, A2.

Shakespeare perform Canale's pious work. There's another shift here: not only from author to text but from text to audience. For Heminge and Condell, it is *readers* who have been 'abused with diverse stolne, and surreptitious copies', and such abuse must end. The perfection of bodily limbs as well as 'numbers' or metre that is augured in the final line conveys wholeness, and the reader has the right to know that the book they hold in their hands is healthy, and complete. As Margreta de Grazia argues, 'the task of the 1623 publication was to unify the disparate and stabilize the transitory' – in a way that creates a veritable family not unlike that imagined by Ovid as he dreams of his library. For, as de Grazia continues, the plays 'are bound to one another by ... natural and legal ties that establish their literal affiliation or consanguinity'.[106]

It is not just the business of print that produces a corrupt text (and one may justly wonder which playscript is authentic, or if any playscript can ever be – a question that has long fuelled Shakespeare studies).[107] Unauthorized or poorly transcribed manuscripts were not rare in the classical or medieval world, as Erasmus discovered with the great Christian scholar Jerome. Through the work of editing Jerome's letters, Erasmus would embrace Jerome as a friend. And friends, as Kathy Eden observes, citing the proverb that opened Erasmus's enormous work, his *Adages*, 'share all things in common'.[108] As he rescued Jerome from 'the monsters of error', doing more than Hercules 'in abolishing so many thousand blunders', Erasmus can ask his patron William Warham in his dedicatory preface to the letters, 'why should not I myself claim a proprietary right in the works of Jerome?'[109] Given the miserable fate to which they were exposed for over a millennium, those works had become 'abandoned goods' – *derelictos*, existing literally in a vacuum and hence, as Erasmus's modern translator interprets the Latin 'in vacuum', 'ownerless'.[110] As Jerome's manuscripts circulated, uncared for, they were no longer recognizable as Jerome's. Erasmus restores the text *to* his new friend, bringing Jerome closer to himself and to others, while not hesitating to claim a right to that work. Intriguingly, Erasmus notes, Jerome did the same, both as editor and as translator – roles Erasmus also revelled in. 'In this line of business Jerome himself has laid down a principle for me in his

---

[106] De Grazia 1991, p. 32; for a counterargument, see Marino 2013, p. 142 on Heminge and Condell's cunning substitutions of themselves for Shakespeare, actors that they were. On the question as to how a play becomes a work, Orgel 2023, pp. 68–97.

[107] See essays in Cox and Kastan 1997.

[108] Eden 2001, p. 4. Eden argues that Erasmus arranged his *Adages* so as to remind the reader both of the 'material property' they are holding and of 'the complex issues of ownership that attach to the intellectual property therein'; p. 163.

[109] Erasmus 1976, Letter 396 to William Warham; Vol. 3, p. 336. On Erasmian claims to ownership here and elsewhere in his work, Jardine 2014, esp. chapter 6, and Pfeiffer 2022, chapter 2. For the often unsung role of his scribes, see Blair 2019.

[110] Erasmus 2012, Letter 396 to William Warham, p. 220.

preface to the books of Kings, repeatedly calling that work his,[111] because anything that we have made our own by correcting, reading, constant devotion, we can fairly claim is ours'[112] – even as Erasmus adds that he has done so only in order to 'reclaim' Jerome for theology.

Asserui is Erasmus's word for reclaim, but it also means to liberate. And what Erasmus frees is, hyperbolically put, 'a river of gold', less hyperbolically, 'a well-stocked library' (265). Like the preface a century later by Shakespeare's 'Friends', the insinuation here, as Eden notes, is that 'only by using his edition, whose purification cost the editor so much labor, does the reader acquire Jerome and no one else' (171). These 'boldly legal terms' allow Erasmus to 'predict the collision between two kinds of profit': that of the humanist-scholar through his investment in past works and that which 'comes increasingly to be expected by purveyors of literary property' (173). Thus does Erasmus utter a challenge for others to do the same: 'I only wish that all good scholars would devote all their forces to the task of restoring as far as possible to its original purity (potest pristinae integritati restituatur) whatever in the way of good authors has some-how survived after such numerous shipwrecks!' (266). Now integral and pristine, those *reliquiae* or relics from the past have been saved from disaster.[113] Now it's up to Erasmus's contemporaries to rescue others' shipwrecked texts.

Rescuing abandoned texts, giving shelter to wandering vagabonds: this was work that, as Jerome demonstrated, was central to translators as well as editors. In many cases, those two skills were combined. In one of early modernity's first treatises on translation – more letter than treatise – Leonardo Bruni anticipates Erasmus's attacks on corrupt manuscripts, but in the form of what he considers corrupt translations. In *De interpretatione recta*, a defence of his recent transla-tion of Aristotle's *Nicomachean Ethics* into Latin, Bruni castigates earlier translators from the Greek such as the scholastic Robert Grosseteste. 'This is not translation, it is confusion; this brings not light, but darkness', in no small part because Grosseteste retained so many Greek words.[114] Bruni goes on to imagine that Aristotle from his spot in the underworld – should he have any knowledge of 'our doings' – 'is surely pained and angry that his books have been so mangled by the ignorant, surely eager to deny his authorship, and surely

---

[111] 'Therefore, first read my Samuel and Malachim; mine, I say, mine. For whatever we have learned and know by often translating and carefully correcting is ours.' (The Latin sounds more assertive, with three repetitions of *meum*: 'Lege ergo primum, Samuel, et Malachim meum: meum, inquam, meum'); Jerome, Preface.

[112] Erasmus 1976 Vol. 3, p. 265; Erasmus 2012, p. 220.

[113] Jardine 2014, p. 58: Erasmus, 'like his hero Jerome before him, is *castigator*, restoring a text damaged by the passage of time to its original, pristine state'.

[114] Bruni 1997, p. 229.

infuriated that they have used his name'.[115] Bruni instead seeks to dispense with darkness. He famously says at the end of his translation of one of Basil's orations, 'Let us now listen to Basil' (Et iam Basilium ipsum audiamus) and at the end of his dedicatory letter to (the pseudo-) Aristotle's *Economics*, 'now let us approach Aristotle's text' (nunc ad textum Aristotelis veniamus).[116] It is Basil we are hearing; it is Aristotle's text arriving before us, as we imagine Aristotle rejoicing in the underworld.

Bruni envisions texts connected to their writers. Good translators must seek to capture the 'majesty of the original author', a *maiestas* threatened by the ignorance of theologians such as Grosseteste, whose (mis)translation of the *Nicomachean Ethics* prompted Bruni to write his own translation in the first place.[117] Bruni's Ciceronian Latin releases Aristotle from the hardened grip of the scholastics, freeing him to become what he has always been: in Bruni's rendering, an orator in the spirit of Demosthenes or a philosopher comfortable in the realm of the spoken word. This is no child of Aristotle's that has been besmirched by supposed teachers of theology whose Latin is virtually incomprehensible. This is Aristotle himself. Bruni's own interest in biography and in the historical contextualization of Florentine authors – namely, Dante, Petrarch, and Boccaccio – shows his commitment to understanding the author through their texts, a connection long minimized. The orphaned, deformed, 'expos'd' text becomes paradigmatic of the orphaned writer, exiled from his own meanings, now to be restored via Bruni's vibrant Latin. Or as he refers to himself, 'I, who am Latin (ego Latinus), do not understand this barbaric talk of you [Scholastics]'.[118]

At the same time, Bruni's Latin grants Aristotle and Plato and Basil a home which they would not have recognized: fifteenth-century Florence, dependent on the public Latin orations of chancellors like Coluccio Salutati and Bruni to preserve it from despots. If a century later Erasmus would make his proprietary claims over Jerome's letters explicit, Bruni makes no such claim. This is Aristotle's text, not his. Still, Erasmus's gesture to reclaim the real Jerome by way of his patient labours reminds us of the mediation that he as editor is performing, one that has the readers ever in mind: those scholars who will follow his lead in rescuing other mutilated texts. Yet as Erasmus revises flawed editions of Jerome's letters, he grants those letters a new life in effectively a new language: a better Latin, one he assumes to have been Jerome's original Latin, too often perverted by scholastics who used the *wrong* Latin for translating Aristotle. That Bruni excelled in the Latin of republican Rome – the model of

---

[115] Ibid.   [116] Bruni 2004, pp. 234, 263.

[117] Bruni 2004, *De interpretatione recta* par. 13, p. 84; Bruni 1987, p. 220.

[118] Bruni 2004, *De interpretatione recta* par. 33, p. 106; Bruni 1987, p. 224.

Florence to which he and others were committed, even as Florence was edging closer and closer to an oligarchy during Bruni's lifetime (and occasionally with Bruni's help)[119] – meant that, even more dramatically than in the case of Erasmus, he was giving Aristotle a voice that contemporary readers similarly skilled in their Cicero could 'hear' and emulate.

But it was a voice that had never been Aristotle's. Never mind that Aristotle didn't know Latin; he was hardly an orator, and his works are dry, logic-driven notes from a classroom. Moreover, he had not been part of the Athenian republic glorified by Florentines like Bruni, to say nothing of Cicero's doomed Roman republic. Yet by having Aristotle speak not like a theologian but as an orator, Bruni makes him especially receptive to those who sought to create a Florence open to exiles and orphans from the past so they could meet up with one another and introduce themselves anew to a receptive audience of scholars trained, like Bruni and Salutati, in Greek as well as Latin: 'let us now listen to Basil'. They, in addition to their texts, are safely 'fostered' after having been mutilated and effectively abandoned by incompetent scholastic translators, referred to as barbarians by Bruni. (The allusion to invasion is surely not accidental: just as Bruni and his contemporaries took pride in Florence's fortunate escape from the invasive Lombards in 1402 – when Visconti was the barbarian at the gate – so can they now boast of having 'preserved' the 'majesty' of the Greeks by keeping them within a Florence committed to preserving liberty.)

Translation into Latin lets the Greeks live. But in turning Aristotle's academic Greek fashioned for young students into Cicero's Latin, Bruni was turning Aristotle into something he was certainly not. This is the only way Bruni felt he could be grasped in a time and place that called on oratorical skills idealizing the moment of Athenian autonomy – two centuries before Aristotle, an emperor's philosopher, was born. This is not necessarily viewed as a detraction by Bruni's contemporaries (save for the theologians) or by those like Poliziano who came later. We have already seen the poem the Greek Herodian 'composed' to praise his Latin translator: 'I can [now] travel more broadly and come into the hands of more people': 'Ut posthac mihi latius vagari, / In plures liceat manus venire'.[120] The wandering inherent in the Latin *vagari* is linked to what Herodian/Poliziano calls the rebirth of history (Felix historiae fide renatae), and he predicts, 'one day the Republic of Latin shall rise'. Herodian himself is reborn. Now fluent in Latin, the gift given him (donatus) by Poliziano, he becomes known to people who speak that language. And yet as Herodian speaks in a metre, not to mention

---

[119] See Najemy 2006, pp. 200–9, for an account of Bruni's less than whole-hearted endorsement of republicanism.

[120] Poliziano 2019, CXXIX: 'Having been given the gift of fluency in Latin by Poliziano, Herodian composes a . . . poem in praise of his translator'; pp. 168–9.

a language, that was never his own (and in any case he wrote prose, not poetry), there is the keen sense that thanks to what has been called the 'inquietudine' or restlessness of early modern humanists, the only way to capture an old language is to force it to become new, so it can keep travelling and be saved from ruin.[121]

Hence the tension between restoring the linguistic perfection of the ancients and adapting to modern use. This was a dynamic which the emergence of European vernaculars, revealed to be dependent not so much on fixity but on change, could only facilitate.[122] There are few better examples of this dynamic of wandering texts and authors than Castiglione's *Cortegiano*, translated into English by Thomas Hoby in the mid 1550s. Vittoria Colonna's unauthorized circulation of Castiglione's *Courtier* has already been noted. Shortly after Castiglione himself tended to its publication, it was translated into French, Spanish, and Polish.[123] But it took almost three decades before its first complete English translation appeared. Hoby characterizes the *Courtier* as one who 'hath long straid about this realme, and the fruite of him either little, or unperfectly received to the commune benefite: for either men skilful in his tunge have delited in him for their owne private commoditie, or elles he hath eftsones spoken in peecemeale by an interpreter.'[124] Thanks to Hoby's solicitude, 'beside his three principal languages, in the which he hath a long tyme haunted all the Courtes of Christendome, hee is [now] become an Englishman (whiche many a longe tyme have wyshed, but fewe attempted and none atchieved) and wel-wiling to dwell in the Court of Englande, and in plight to tel his own cause' (A.iii). In his modest prefatory remarks to a translation strikingly close to the Italian, both lexically and syntactically, and absent of copious additions or commentary, Hoby goes on to say as much. '[The Courtier] can so well speak for himself, and answere to the opinion men have a long time conceived of him, that whatsoever I shoulde write therein, were but labour in waste' (A.iii). There is no need for the self-effacing Hoby to elaborate on his work as translator; we are hearing the Courtier as he is. This 'strai', to use Hoby's verb as a noun, has made it to a new home, where others can welcome him.

Far from being simply celebratory, however, Hoby's words about one of early modern Europe's most popular works contain a hint of darkness, as he alludes to the spectre of a ghost that has been 'haunt[ing] all the Courtes of Christendome'. As Loredana Polezzi notes, 'Translation takes place not just when words move

---

[121] See Cacciari 2019, *La mente inquieta: Saggio sull'Umanesimo* (*The Unquiet Mind: A Study in Humanism*).

[122] Arrigoni 2019 comments on the 'necessary death and rebirth of words' implied by Dante's 'living' if fragile vernacular and the contrast with 'the perpetual and non-corruptible' language of Latin; p. 189.

[123] Burke 2002.

[124] Castiglione 1561, A.iii., 'To the right honorable the Lord Henry Hastinges'.

on their own, but also, and mostly, when people move'.[125] Hoby became proficient in Italian not only because he was drawn to the language while in school but because he was forced to leave England in the 1550s when the Catholic Mary Tudor – the so-called Bloody Mary – became queen. The straying Castiglione was also the straying Protestant Thomas Hoby, who completed his translation in 1556 while in Europe, publishing it only in 1561 when he was back in England, safe under Elizabeth's reign.

Much can be said about a Catholic Castiglione coming to England in the guise of a Protestant as regards the precariousness of the translator himself. It's not clear to what extent Hoby felt welcomed in Italy, but one might speculate that his return to England with the Courtier in tow is his way of giving back – paradoxically, perhaps, given Italy's status as a Catholic country (and Hoby pointedly sidesteps the religious divide when he remarks on the Courtier haunting 'all the Courtes of Christendome'). Abigail Brundin notes that Hoby marked many of his books with the Latin motto 'Tendit in ardua virtus' ('Virtue strives for what is difficult').[126] The phrase is from the final work of an Ovid still in exile, *Epistulae ex Ponto* (II.2.111), and may have been Hoby's way of expressing his desire to challenge himself intellectually. But it could also have alluded to the religious persecution following Mary's accession. Hoby's preface opens referring to another exile: the general and politician Themistocles, who, despite his successes in battle, was ultimately ostracized by the Athenians and forced to leave – and who turned to his former enemies, the Persians, for asylum. He then 'demaunded respite to learne the Persian tunge to tell his owne cause' – a cause, which Hoby goes on to say, is precisely what the Courtier is now in a position to tell Englishmen (A.iii). Here it is Castiglione's work that needs to learn a new 'tunge'. But the Hoby who succeeded in teaching the Courtier the language of his new court also had to presumably tell his own cause while in Italy.

Will the Courtier ever go home? And where is Castiglione in all of this? The notion of an absolute departure from one's home, the being 'made over' into an Englishman, or a Spaniard or Frenchman, may exhibit the quiet confidence of the translator. But even as it affirms the process of appropriation that accompanies translation, to use Anne Coldiron's phrase,[127] it also suggests another way of thinking about how editors and translators conceived their roles. They create contexts in which a work will be received and understood; they give it a home where it can become familiar to those who could not have encountered it

---

[125] Polezzi 2012, p. 348.

[126] From the 2019 Cambridge exhibit, 'Cultures in Translation', https://exhibitions.lib.cam.ac.uk/hoby/.

[127] See Coldiron's comments on Hoby's 'aim to English the *Cortegiano* as an appropriated *Courtyer*'; Coldiron 2015, p. 165.

otherwise. This is what Bruni arguably attempted to do with his Latin translations of Aristotle, even as he argues that he has captured Aristotle's personal
style in ways unavailable to Grosseteste. Castiglione is left largely unre-
marked on in Hoby's preface, and that absence is telling. Unlike the future
Heminge and Condell, Hoby does not refer to his translated text as an orphan.
But he does emphasize its former lack of attachment to an English home, and
as a stray it was displaced and in need. There *is* no return to its now-dead
author, no back-and-forth: only moving on, thanks to the labours – and
compassion – of others.

This is a line of thinking intimated by Castiglione himself, as may be seen in his
own view of his text. It wasn't expressed in response to an impudent Colonna
eager to get the *Cortegiano* into others' hands but in the context of his remarks on
the Italian language, which – far from needing to be grounded in the 'dead'
tongues of poets such as Petrarch – should be based in *usus* or use, ever changing
as spoken language always is. Given that the *Cortegiano* is nothing if not
a dialogue, and hence the sharing of language as spoken in real time by gentlemen
and gentlewomen from throughout the Italian peninsula, Castiglione's conviction
as expressed in his prefatory send-off (once he finishes complaining about
Colonna) is worthy of consideration. 'The power and true role of good speech
consists more in usage than in anything else, and it is always bad to employ words
that are not in use' (La forza e vera regula del parlar bene consiste più nell'uso che
in altro, e sempre è vizio usar parole che non siano in consuetudine).[128] Conte
Ludovico Canossa, who stands in for Castiglione's personal views in Book I, will
argue that the force of habit is responsible for the life and death of words and
languages themselves. Some words lose their grace after time, others gain force
and acquire both 'grace and dignity' (grazie e dignità) – until 'the envious jaws of
time' take them to their death (I.36).[129] Castiglione clarifies what the consummate
philologists Bruni and, perhaps less so, Poliziano obscure: languages change, and
words and works need to be reborn – but differently, and through the ennobling
work of others. As the Conte reminds us, 'in the end, we and all our things are
mortal'. This includes Castiglione's own book, along with the author himself, an
author open to the necessity of rewriting and replacing, in order to situate his
words in new moments and new contexts – work he painstakingly did as he
revised the *Cortegiano* for over a decade.

---

[128] Castiglione 1959, p. 4; Castiglione 1991, p. 5.
[129] Castiglione 1959, p. 58; Castiglione 1991, p. 76. The sentiment owes much to Horace's *Ars
poetica*, 60–2: 'As forests change their leaves with each year's decline, and the earliest drop off:
so with words, the old race dies, and, like the young of human kind, the new-born bloom and
thrive'; and elsewhere, 'look to life and manners for a model, and draw from living words'
(318–19); Horace 2014, pp. 455, 477.

But it is the Courtier who has haunted the courts, not Castiglione. One might remark on the extent to which courtiership was a profession that left its practitioners ever vulnerable in a world dependent on patronage and thus on others' good graces. The patronus – originating in *pater* – was sought out like an adoptive father by talented figures in need of a home, not unlike the orphaned book or the orphan Poliziano. Even Castiglione, a count and member of a family of albeit minor nobility, had to solicit patrons during his lifetime so he could serve as a diplomat, advisor, and, on occasion, poet. The stray could also be the man, albeit the man that Hoby, himself a temporary exile, largely ignores.

Another wanderer who took it upon himself to 'foster father', as he put it, texts that had left their homes was the translator John Florio. His parents were Italian Protestants who came to England when it had a Protestant king. Like Hoby, they left when it became Catholic and then returned.[130] Not only bilingual but trilingual, Florio went from compiling the first Italian–English dictionary, his enormous *Worlde of Words*, to translating an equally enormous work mentioned earlier in this section, Montaigne's *Essais*. While the translation was apparently done at the urgent request of several 'ladies', there is something in the nature of Montaigne's project that connects Florio's choice to Hoby's – and to the world of editors and translators intervening for others and for one another.

Florio's Montaigne opens with two dedicatory letters – more on those in a bit – while Montaigne 'proper' appears in the short, pithy 'Au Lecteur', in which the writer famously declares that were he living in more 'primitive' times, he would have portrayed himself 'tout nue'. Before introducing his wished-for but unachieved portrait, he states, clearly and forthrightly, his aim for his book, for which 'je ne m'y suis proposé alcune fin que domestique et privee'.[131] Or in Florio's rather contorted rendering, 'I have proposed unto myself no other than a familiar and private end'.[132] Surely 'familiar' is a viable synonym insofar as it corresponds to 'domestique', derived from domus or household, and thus a place of family. While this process of familiarization intimates that we are being let into Montaigne's 'domestic' space, there is also the reverse at work. Montaigne explicitly invites himself as guest into our 'private' space by way of his book. How willing are we to make him familiar to us, whether it be in French or Florio's English?[133]

These are the family dynamics that Florio addresses in his dedicatory epistle to two 'most-Honored Ladies', Lucie, Countess of Bedford, and her mother, and he calls attention to the oddity of this dual dedication: 'Strange it may seeme to

---

[130] See a stunning introduction to Florio in Wyatt 2003, pp. 152–254.

[131] Montaigne 1962, Vol. I, p. 1.   [132] Montaigne 1603, A6v.

[133] Much of Montaigne's work is arguably an attempt to 'familiarize' – to enable himself, and 'par accident', his readers – with the new and the strange.

some, whose seeming is mis-seeming, in one worthlesse patronage to joyne two
so severallie all-worthy Ladies' – going on in his typically over-the-top language of flattery.[134] If Castiglione's Courtier is the young (male) ghost who
haunts the courts and is now 'straid' to England, Florio's Montaigne is a young
girl, since all translations are reputed as female, delivered at 'second hand' – an
allusion to the inferiority of the female sex that hardly seems appropriate given
the dedicatees. And he is this foundling's 'foster-father', who

> having transported it from *France* to *England*; put it in English clothes; taught
> it to talke our tongue (though many-times with a jerke of the French *Iargon*)
> would set it forth to the best service I might... Yet hath it this above your
> other servants: it may not onely serve you two, to repeate in true English what
> you reade in fine French, but many thousands more, to tell them in their owne,
> what they would be taught in an other language. (A2)

The book is going through its own process of adoption. Transported to a new
family, dressed and educated, she is now sent out as a serving-woman to work as
a tutor or teacher, per the trajectory of so many Renaissance orphans as
illuminated in John Boswell's work.

But there is more to this story. One of the editions of Montaigne's *Essais* that
Florio consulted for his massive project likewise references a foster-father. The
title page to the 1595 edition specifies that it incorporates material found after the
author's death three years earlier, making the *Essais* now a third longer than earlier
versions (*Edition nouuelle, trouuee apres le deceds de l'autheur / reueuë &
augmentee par luy d'un tiers plus qu'aux precedentes impressions*). A lengthy
dedication follows, written by a woman who called herself Montaigne's 'fille de
alliance' or adoptive daughter, Marie le Jars de Gournay. Gournay had been so
taken by the *Essais* when she first read them that she sent Montaigne numerous
letters begging him to let her meet him; indeed, in the fall of 1588, Montaigne
made an extended visit to her family home in Gournay-sur-Aronde, in Picardy.[135]
She wrote a novel based on his sojourn there and evidently stayed in contact with
Montaigne, though surprisingly she did not learn of his death until a year later,
suggesting that the bond was not as tight as she may have believed. Still, they were
close enough for Montaigne's widow to have sent Gournay the 1588 edition of the
Essais with Montaigne's extensive marginal notations, and to support Gournay's
publication of the 1595 *Edition nouuelle* much amplified. Gournay is explicitly
mentioned in that amplified text, when Montaigne refers to his 'fille d'alliance'
(although the passage's authenticity is disputed by scholars).[136] But she is

---

[134] Montaigne 1603, A2.   [135] Gournay 1998, p. 6.

[136] The closing pages of 'De la presumption' (On Presumption'), *Essais* 2.17, include an extensive
paragraph on Gournay, 'ma fille d'alliance', referencing her sincerity, affection, and, especially,
her excellent 'jugement' of the *Essais*; Montaigne 1962, Vol. II, p. 66.

everywhere present in her long dedication, recalling her closeness to her 'patre d'alliance', his love for her and his trust in her work, and in turn, the trust of his widow. Indeed, thanks to his widow's gift of the *Essais* with her husband's notes, Gournay can 'restore to him a new appearance of life (restituer un nouvel image de vie) by the continuation of the friendship that he bore me'.[137] The book becomes hers as well, as she defends this version of the *Essais* from others that have appeared in Lyon and elsewhere since Montagne's death, the result of greedy printers having 'scrapped, truncated, and exploited' the original, 'less concerned' with accuracy than with making money.[138]

Yet the 1595 edition provoked what Philippe Desan has called a 'true editorial tempest' – in no small part because of its bold preface.[139] Gournay opens her 1598 edition announcing that she has 'retracted' what in the 1595 preface represented little more than 'the blindness of youth' ('te confesse que ie me retracte de cette Preface que l'aveuglement de mon aage') (Figure 1).[140] Which is to say, she retracted everything. The new preface is a mere four sentences, shorter than Montaigne's 'Au lecteur', which appears on the following page. Interestingly, John Florio, who obviously consulted both Gournay's 1595 and 1598 editions – the latter absent its manifesto – chided this 'fille d'alliance' for having removed her strong words. In his aforementioned dedication to his two female patrons, he writes, 'how worthily qualified, embellished, furnished [this book] is, let his faire-spoken, and fine-witted Daughter by alliance passe her verdict, which shee need not recant' (A2). But she had, of course, recanted. She would resurface only in 1635, with a dedication to Richelieu in which she now speaks of Montaigne's text, rather than herself, as the 'adopted' child or 'orpheline'.[141] The true protector has become Richelieu; and in any case, the lengthy life story from the original 1595 edition is still omitted, to be restored only shortly before Gournay's death in 1645.

Florio's circuitous allusions to himself as a wanderer in need of support in his own preface remind us of his tenuous circumstances as a teacher and courtier dependent on others' favours.[142] If the 'adoptive daughter' is the *Essais* and Marie de Gournay alike, Florio is both foster father and adoptive son, having wandered between cultures to familiarize 'thousands' with the strangeness that is Montaigne. But he becomes more than that in the second, 1613 edition of the *Essais*. If the title

---

[137] Gournay 1998, 30–1.   [138] Desan and Coulombel 1995, p. 15.
[139] Desan and Coulombel 1995, p. 16.   [140] Montagne 1598: n.p.
[141] Desan 2003, p. 309, who also cites the 1635 edition in which Gournay speaks of 'cet orpheline qui m'étoit commis', i.e., the *Essais* themselves.
[142] Particularly telling is his citation in the dedicatory letter of a well-known phrase from Torquato Tasso's *Gerusalemme liberata*, to be discussed in Section 3, where the narrator refers to himself as a *peregrino errante* (wandering pilgrim) asking for Alfonso d'Este's hospitality. Florio changes the passage to indicate that he has the good fortune to find himself in a '*porto di salute e pace*', a harbor of well-being (A3v).

Figure 1 Marie de Gournay, Preface, Montaigne's *Essais*, Paris, 1598, courtesy Beinecke Library.

page of 1603 omitted any mention of the translator, Florio's name is how prominently featured, with significantly more space devoted to his credentials than to Montaigne's (Figure 2). More importantly, the edition features a full-page engraving of Florio (Figure 3) from his (revised, 1611) Italian dictionary, now called *Queen Anna's New World of Words* – a homage to England's queen, who has now become Florio's patron. As Peter Stallybrass observes, 'the author has been displaced by the translator. It is Florio, not Montaigne, who gazes out at the reader.'[143] A dedication to the queen follows, as well as verses by admirers of Florio's work, including Samuel Daniel, one of England's leading poets at the time. And since pictures are worth a thousand words, Florio's own 'Au lecteur' now has him saying far less than he did earlier. He opens with the brusque 'Enough, if not

---

[143] Stallybrass 2011, p. 211. Rizzi 2017 notes that translators' portraits allow them 'to *become* the context that authoritatively informs the translation and the network that is supporting its production and reception'; p. 42.

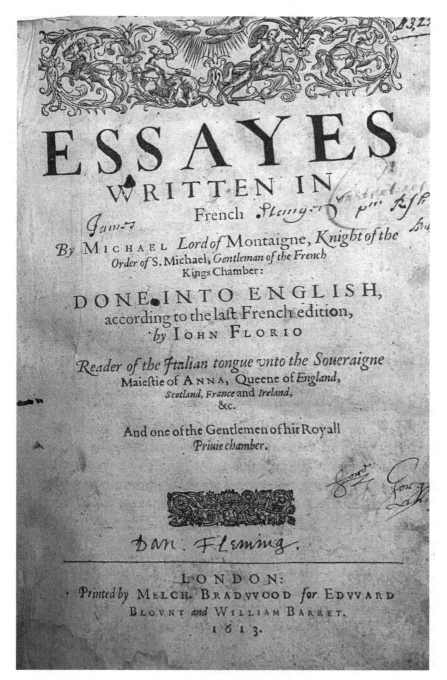

Figure 2 Title page, John Florio's translation of Montaigne's *Essayes*, London, 1613, courtesy Beinecke Library.

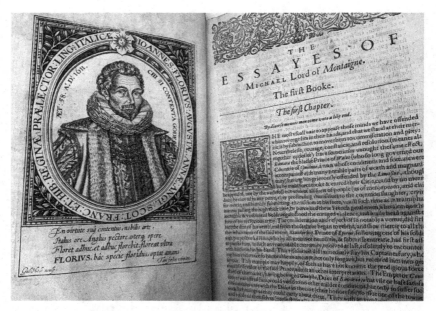

Figure 3 John Hole, engraving of John Florio, *The Essayes of Michael Lord of Montaigne*, London, 1613, courtesy Beinecke Library.

too much, hath been sayd of this Translation' by others and, in the earlier volume, by himself. But he ends his brisk, three-sentence 'Advertissement' with an allusion, his last ever, to Marie de Gournay: 'Let me conclude with this worthie mans daughter of alliance: *Que t'en semble donc lecteur?*' – So what does this seem like to you, reader?[144] This is the very question with which Gournay closed her short 'Preface sur les Essais de Michel Seigneur de Montaigne, par sa Fille d'Alliance' in 1598. Rather than give readers her long defence of Montaigne as well as of herself, she now offers them 'nothing more than my ears, so I can hear your opinion of this book. So what does it seem like to you, reader?'[145]

As he echoes Montaigne's 'Fille d'Alliance', Florio arguably creates a sense of true *alliance* between himself and other foster children, who themselves became foster parents, tutors, protectors. Florio's tumultuous childhood, his double belonging, and, perhaps, his non-belonging, served him well in negotiating between three languages and two cultures. His frontispiece attests to the success he has known since the first edition of the *Essais* appeared in 1603: he is now the 'Praelector Ling: Italice' to 'Anne, Angl: Scot: Franc: et Hib Regina', Italian teacher to the Queen. Or, as Michael Wyatt observes, 'a man at the top of his game'.[146] Little wonder that as he chose to feature his portrait instead of Montaigne's, he invoked

---

[144] Montaigne 1613: A3, 'To the Reader.'   [145] Montaigne 1598, A.   [146] Wyatt 2005, p. 252.

the never-named Gournay, still wishing, a decade later, that she had retained her distinctive defence introducing the *Essais* rather than ceding her 'place' to others.[147] At the same time, even as Florio defends his soeur d'alliance, he fails to translate her (admittedly lengthy) preface, and she remains a 'strai' in England.

At roughly this same moment in nearby Spain, Miguel de Cervantes was referring to himself not as the *padre* but as the 'padrasto' or stepfather of *Don Quijote* – a manuscript translated into Castilian, from the Arabic, by a Morisco from Toledo. Since he is not the *padre*, Cervantes will thus not 'implore you, . . . dearest reader, to pardon or ignore the faults you see in this child of mine' ('en este mi hijo').[148] Is the translator, then, the true father of this troubled child? And yet the story wasn't quite over. Cervantes would be less coy about his relationship to his words in his sequel to the *Quijote* – a sequel in part prompted by the publication of a second part to *Don Quijote* by a writer masquerading as Cervantes. Even as he tells his readers that he's not going to go out of his way to insult his plagiarist, he declares at the end of his preface, 'this second part of *Don Quixote* that I'm offering you is cut by the same craftsman (artífice) and from the cloth as the first one, and . . . in it I give you Don Quixote prolonged and finally dead and buried, so that nobody can presume to produce any more evidence against him' (porque ninguno se atreva a levantarle nuevos testimonios).[149] Artisan if not father, Cervantes engages in the brutal act of killing off his creation, although it certainly would not prevent future translators from writing their own versions of a sequel.

3 *Revenants:* When Stolen Words Come Back

Marie de Gournay probably never saw the 1613 *Essayes* where Florio repeats her question, in French – what does it all mean, lecteur? But we do know that Montaigne saw the three editions of his *Essais* (1580, 1585, 1588), rereading and expanding them through additions and new essays (despite the extraction of La Boétie's poems from the 1588 edition, deletions were relatively rare). As he saw his words in print, Montaigne came to reflect – not unlike Derrida – on his distance from them, and in a marginal note published in Marie de Gournay's 1595 edition, he muses that even though he has given to his book as 'purely and irrevocably as any man can give . . . to his own corporal children', 'that little good which I have done him is no longer in my disposition. He may know many things that myself know no longer and hold of me what I could not hold myself and which (if need should require) I must borrow of him as of a stranger' (estranger) – in Florio's translation.[150] Might this perhaps

---

[147] Gournay's disappearing act ensured that, following her death, 'the celebrated masterpiece of her "father" was virtually severed from her name'; Gournay 1998, p. 1.

[148] Chartier 1994, p. 45.   [149] Cervantes 2001, p. 486; Cervantes 2010, p. 392.

[150] 'Affection of Fathers for their Children'. *Essais* 2.8; Montaigne 1962, Vol. I, p. 442; Montaigne 1603, p. 223.

uneasy encounter with a work he once sent out and no longer recognizes, the content of which he no longer remembers, explain why Montaigne went back, continuously, even obsessively, to read, reread, and add to his already published text, scribbling in the margins or dictating to a scribe? Such additions may have been one way of making this strange work his own again as he perfected what George Hoffman calls the 'separate genre' of 'the rewrite':[151] re-familiarizing, re-domesticating it, only to see it go out again and become once more a stranger.

Montaigne was hardly the only early modern author who went back to his books once they were printed. While few were as explicit as Montaigne about the meaning of that return, the propensity of early modern authors to revisit their published texts is noteworthy. Ludovico Ariosto is one prominent example. The rare author from the sixteenth century to whom (temporary) copyright privileges were granted, his *Orlando furioso* consisted of forty cantos in 1516. He made considerable lexical and stylistic changes for the 1521 re-edition, then expanded the poem to forty-six cantos in 1532. Erasmus's equally popular *Adages* provide another example. The author continually added proverbs, describing 'each new expansion as an effort to "enrich" his collection',[152] which grew over three decades from 800 to some 4,000 – five times the size of the original text. Erasmus's ongoing labours are understandable in light of the project itself, aimed at being encyclopaedic; Ariosto's are somewhat less so, despite the seemingly encyclopaedic range of his poem. To what extent was he too trying to make his work familiar – once again *his*, already a challenge given that his *Orlando furioso* was a continuation of the earlier, incomplete *Orlando innamorato* of Matteo Maria Boiardo? At the same time, the process of print enabled, even encouraged, these returns and revisions; it doesn't necessarily mandate an act of finality or completion. Whereas manuscript circulation hardly precluded going back to one's work, the existence of numerous printers, who (especially when dealing with a bestseller) hoped to make a profit through updated versions, encouraged authors to revise.[153] Erasmus used his own cultural capital as well as his itinerancy to approach different printers in different cities who might do the job more quickly, enabling him to reach new audiences. His 1508 *Adages* were published by Aldus Manutius; the revised 1513 edition appeared with the press of Johann Froben in Basel, during Erasmus's stay in the city – and after a pirated edition had appeared.[154]

---

[151] Hoffman 1998, p. 129. Hoffman also argues for the importance of expiring publishing privileges, given that Montaigne had an eight-year privilege for the 1580 *Essais* and was well aware of 'the legal criteria of a new work'; p. 128. On Montaigne's conceptions of ownership, see Green 2012, pp. 89–140.

[152] Eden 2001, p. 4.

[153] For specifics, see Pettegree 2010, chapter 4, 'The Creation of a European Book Market', pp. 65–90.

[154] On the *Adages* and its editions, see Phillips 1964. Eden 2001, p. 142, asserts that Erasmus's book 'helped to secure the fame and fortune' of both Aldus's and Froben's publishing houses.

Of course – as Ariosto's attempts to obtain fairly limited copyright privileges suggest – the printers often did what they wished without the author's licence; a published text was rarely the author's from a legal point of view.[155] But printers and translators too indulged in the fantasy of returning texts to authors. While Aldus Manutius dedicated much of his career to publishing dead writers from the distant past, he also took up more recent ones, such as Giovanni Pontano, who passed away while his book was in press. But working with living authors like Erasmus could prompt a different kind of relationship. In his preface to a treatise on hunting by one Cardinal Adriano Castellesi, Aldus explains that the manuscript arrived in his hands as a gift, one he quickly considered 'worthy of being printed in our type'. But, he goes on, 'because I thought it missed you [Castellesi] as deeply as a daughter misses her parent, I am sending it back to you (remitto eam ad te), adorned (ornatam) in the finest garment that I could provide. You will recognize it as yours, and in it the warm feelings of your friend Aldus for you.'[156] 'Tu tuam recognosces': an undoing of Poliziano's jibe to Paul. Yet this *filia* who has been reunited with her father is now appropriately dressed in the 'handsome typeface' of Aldus's text.[157] The word 'ornatam' takes us back to medieval poets' requests for a 'gentil cor', which Aldus has now become.

This is not, in other words, the simple return of the book to its author as imagined by Spenser. It's not clear whether Castellesi knew that his manuscript had even arrived in Aldus's shop. We saw the complications that arose when Sannazaro's *Arcadia* was published without its author's knowledge, prompting Sannazaro to write two additional chapters and a goodbye to his bagpipe in 1504. A decade later, Aldus himself decided to invest in what had become this popular tale of an exiled, lovesick Neapolitan dwelling among shepherds; and he does so by announcing in his preface to Sannazaro that he, Aldus, deserves to be accused of 'temerity and arrogance' for sending 'a gift to someone to whom the gift actually belongs'. Yet he defends himself by insisting that

> although you composed some time ago the learned and eloquent *Arcadia* ... and it belongs to you, as it truly does (et sit illa, ut est, tua) nevertheless somehow when it has been published in this way, it has become my property too (sic edita facta est etiam mea). And so what is mine in this book, I give and dedicate to you.[158]

The cordial preface closes with a citation from one of Virgil's Eclogues – plus an added line by Aldus – and the command that Sannazaro acknowledge or claim

---

[155] On this fascinating legal background, see Putnam 1962, Vol. 2, pp. 345–510, 'The Beginnings of Property in Literature'.

[156] Manutius 2017, pp. 214–15.   [157] My thanks to Jonathan Nelson for the phrase.

[158] Manutius 2017, pp. 226–7. Sannazaro seems to have been aware beforehand of Aldus's plans to republish his work.

this new *Arcadia* as his own: 'Nunc Arcadiam tuam agnosce.' Even if Aldus doesn't invoke the filial metaphor, he asks Sannazaro to take responsibility and become, as dedicatee, the protector of his own text. Surely hovering over this one-way conversation is the reminder that the first *Arcadia* was published without its author's consent. Unlike the original editor, Aldus implies that he has been respectful of the author – even as his by now extremely prestigious press has arguably ennobled the original work, as he comes to own it too.

Would Sannazaro have felt estranged from Aldus's gift, having already – as he put it – left his *sampogna* behind? Would Spenser, who explicitly asked that *The Shepheardes Calender* return to him, acknowledge the bound book in his hands as his own? Like Montaigne, these authors had already given licence for their works to be sent out (or in Sannazaro's creative revision, to stay put while the author left). They were thus facing the consequences of what Sarah Stroup has set out in relationship to a much earlier period, the first century BCE: 'What does it mean to entrust one's text – sometimes conceptualized as one's "persona" – to the care of another?'[159]

This was the question asked in Section 1 of works such as Horace's and Ovid's from the period Stroup references, as the poem necessarily leaves its author (or in Sannazaro's case, the author leaves the poem). The tension between familiarization and estrangement, exacerbated in the era of print that was largely the focus of Section 2, will be especially pronounced here.

Montaigne may have no longer recognized his *Essais* once they were published. But at least he knew they had gone to press. Yet, as happened with Colonna, one's words are sometimes circulated or published without the author's knowledge, a seeming violation of trust that arguably prompts writers to feel estranged from their words – assuming, per Poliziano's jibe, those words are still their own. Particularly in the era of print, when it took publishers considerably less time than scribes to generate multiple copies of a work, how might an author go about taking back something which they hadn't declared ready to send out in the first place, and were they always able to follow Sannazaro's lead? At the same time, is it always true that a reader's decision to publish a text not their own is to be outright condemned? Vittoria Colonna's words would have lingered forever in manuscript if she had had her way (and perhaps, without Colonna, Castiglione's would have shared the same fate). Philippo Pirogallo claims it was less of an error to 'displease one lady (una sola Donna) however rare and great, than to deny so many men (tanti huomini) what they want'.[160] This deliberately plays on the hierarchy of gendered roles, yet might it be the case that certain words deserve to be shared with

---

[159] Stroup 2010, p. 33.   [160] Colonna 2023, pp. 34–5.

readers – and so need to leave their authors' homes, like Horace's *Epistles*? So to three late Renaissance examples.

Polymath, scholar, writer, nun, Sor Juana Inés de la Cruz was one of the most accomplished intellectuals of the seventeenth century. Born of a Spanish father and Mexican mother who never married, she early on demonstrated the desire or 'inclinación' to know.[161] After spending a decade at the viceregal court in Mexico City, she departed for the convent so as to avoid marriage and dedicate herself to writing. By the late 1680s, with the assistance of a devoted female patron, she was publishing poetry, plays, and prose, navigating the legacy of European literature and philosophy with an assurance that reflects detachment from her native heritage to which she nonetheless alluded in several works. But if religious life in the comfortable convent of the Hieronymite nuns gave her the freedom to compile a library of more than 2,000 books and write for the court, it also made her vulnerable to a conservative bishopric that saw her freedom as misguided and irreverent. In her last few years, she largely withdrew from public writings after composing what has become one of her best-known works, her *Respuesta a Sor Filotea*.

Written in 1691, four years before her death from plague at age forty-four, the *Respuesta* is a spirited defence of Sor Juana's literary practice in response to a bishop's complaint. In its pages, she pledges that this is the last time she will defend herself from attack; instead, she will embrace a new 'inclinación': to be silent (de callar).[162] Yet if the withdrawal of this lively, widely published woman would generate a loss, another kind of loss led Sor Juana to write the *Respuesta* in the first place: that of her words, exacerbated by issues of gender and religious constraint as well as geography. She wrote the *Respuesta* following the unauthorized publication of her critique of a sermon delivered forty years earlier by the Portuguese Jesuit Antonio Vieira on the topic of favours (*finezas*) given by Christ. Curiously, the critique was published by none other than Puebla's Bishop Fernández de Santa Cruz, with the new title of *Carta Atenagórica* – words worthy of Athena, an overblown expression of admiration that only dimly conceals the criticisms within. The accompanying letter by the bishop that opens the pamphlet accuses Sor Juana of failing to acknowledge the source of her own *finezas* – that is, God – and of expressing herself in verse and relying on 'pagan' poets and philosophers when she should be focused on Scripture. Fernández moreover disguises his voice as that of one Sor Filotea, as though he was speaking to Sor Juana 'nun to nun' from the Convent of the

---

[161] In her *Respuesta a Sor Filotea*, Sor Juana speaks frequently about this 'inclination' – at one point claiming that 'it has been so great that it has conquered all else!'; Juana Inés de la Cruz 1997, pp. 26–7.

[162] Juana Inés de la Cruz 1997, pp. 68–9. On Sor Juana's strategic use of silence – a silence she promises in the *Respuesta* but continually interrupts – see Bokser 2006.

Santisima Trinidad in Puebla, signing off with 'su afecta servidora', your affectionate (female) servant, Filotea de la Cruz.[163]

But Sor Juana saw through the fiction. Her elegant, complex response is prompted by her anger regarding a text effectively stolen from her after she had entrusted it to the bishop per his request.[164] At the same time, she takes up the modesty topos so common to women – and many men – of her era as she pretends that the reason she is so upset is because the work had no value to start with. She opens claiming to be grateful for this 'unexpected favor' of publication. Incapable of offering sufficient thanks, she can only express her amazement ('admiraciones'), stating, '[when I first saw] that letter you were pleased to dub "Worthy of Athena" – I burst into tears (a thing that does not come easily to me)'.[165] Yet she weeps not only for this favour but because her words were unpolished and unready for print. Invoking the metaphor of the orphaned text, she characterizes herself not as a Poliziano abandoning his child to wild beasts but as the mother of no one other than Moses.

> Could I have foreseen the happy destiny for which it was born – for I cast it out, like a second Moses, as a foundling (*expósita*) upon the waters of the Nile of silence, where it was discovered and cherished by a princess no less than yourself – ... I should first have drowned it with these very hands to which it was born ... But now that the letter's fate has cast it before your doors, a foundling so orphaned (tan expósita y huérfana) that its very name was bestowed by you, I regret that among all its many deformities it displays the defects of hasty composition.[166]

The (feminized) bishop becomes the Pharaoh's daughter who takes in the abandoned child, giving him a new name.

And yet, as Robert McDonald reminds us, Moses is a child whose destiny is well beyond his adoptive mother's control – a comment with implications for Sor Juana's *Respusta*.[167] But let us turn to the adoptive mother who precipitated this response in the first place – and why. In the letter prefacing the *Carta Atenagórica*, the bishop starts off flattering his 'sister' nun. Appropriating her female voice, he claims to have admired the liveliness of her conceits, the intelligence of her proofs, and the *claridad* with which she takes on her subject.[168] And then, these lines:

> So that you may see yourself more suitably reflected in this document (en este papel, Sor Juana's own work) I have had it printed. In this way you may acknowledge the treasures that God has heaped up in your soul, so that just as you possess greater understanding, you may come to feel all the more

---

[163] Juana Inés de la Cruz 2005, p. 253.   [164] For the critical background, see Wray 2017.
[165] Juana, 2009, pp. 40–1.   [166] Juana, 2009, pp. 96–7.   [167] McDonald 1993, pp. 310–11.
[168] Juana 2009, pp. 222–3.

grateful, for gratitude and understanding are always delivered at the same birthing (un mismo parto). (224–5)

The ultimate plan is to ensure a further act of understanding: 'if until now you have employed your talents well, in future you may do so even better' (225).

Philippo Pirogallo had hoped that his publication of Vittoria Colonna's poems would enable her to 'gli . . . rivedere di nuovo' or see them again, and so be moved to correct his poor transcriptions and publish an authoritative volume. Printing another's work as a path towards encouraging them to reflect on their own words when misrepresented by others becomes an interesting way of theorizing the supposed power of print and its mediators. But the bishop's goal is to force Sor Juana to see *herself* in the printed text – as though the handwritten document she originally gave to Fernández did not allow her to see herself objectively within it. The published text becomes a means of separating Sor Juana from her words so as to enable her to acknowledge who she is, and who she is not; 'in this way you may acknowledge the treasures that God has heaped up in your soul' (para que reconozca los tesoros que Dios depositó en su alma). *Reconozca* returns us to the phrase used by Aldus when sending (back) to Cardinal Castellesi his now-published book: 'Tu tuam recognosces' – you'll recognize it as yours. But in acknowledging these words as hers, Sor Juana is being urged to see them as misguided, and she should abandon the poetry 'for which [she has] been so celebrated' and improve herself 'by sometimes reading (leyendo alguna vez) the Book of Jesus Christ' (224–5). Sor Juana has dallied – like Boethius, Justus Lipsius, and especially Jerome – for far too long 'in the study of philosophers and poets; it is now high time for your pastimes to be perfected and your books improved' (227). The letter (almost) ends with an expression of compassion that becomes a threat: 'It is a pity when a person of great understanding stoops to lowly, swindling matters on earth, without longing to decipher what happens in Heaven; but once it rests down on the ground, may it not sink still further, considering what happens in Hell' (229). 'El Infierno' awaits a Sor Juana who refuses to use the real *beneficios* or benefits that God has given her – unless she can acknowledge those gifts and enable 'divine generosity, unstinted, [to] make those benefits greater than ever before' (228–9).

On the surface, the bishop does not chastise Sor Juana for daring to attack a respected theologian. And at least on the surface, Sor Juana expresses gratitude 'for the one who had the letter printed, unbeknownst to me (sin noticia mia), who titled it and underwrote its cost, and who thus honored it, unworthy as it was of all this, on its own account and on account of its author (siendo de todo indigna por sí y por su autora)' (42–3). But then she comes to the true payoff of being able to 'see' herself in the mirror of her text. Its publication has paradoxically given her 'license to speak and plead my case' (44–5). And this *licencia* is comparable to what was once given to a woman from the very Bible to which the bishop is insisting Sor Juana devote more of her attention: Esther, from the biblical book bearing her name. In the full passage:

> Sheltered (debajo) by the assumption that I speak with the safe-conduct guaranteed by your favors and with the warrant bestowed by your goodwill, and by the fact that you, like another Ahasuerus, have allowed me to kiss the tip of the golden scepter of your affection as a sign that you grant me the kind license to speak and to plead my case in your venerable presence, (benévola licencia para hablar y proponer en vuestra venerable presencia) I declare that I have taken to heart your most holy admonition to apply myself to the study of holy scripture. (42–5)

The Book of Esther's eponymous heroine, who concealed her identity as a Hebrew, wrestles with whether or not to go into the chambers of the tyrant Ahasuerus unannounced, and so risk possible death – for no one is allowed to enter his rooms unless expressly invited to do so. Yet Esther, Ahasuerus's wife, has a mission, which is to save the Hebrews from the mass slaughter planned by the king's chief counsellor. She ultimately decides to go in. 'If I perish, I perish', she concludes her speech (Esther 4:16, King James Version). But she does not perish. Ahasuerus's gesture of extending to her his sceptre gives her the freedom not only to set a time for her appeal but to reveal to him, finally, who she is. What could have been punishable on any number of levels is instead permitted, all because Esther was licensed to speak. So does Sor Juana take licence to utter her eloquent respuesta as she describes what she loves: her words and her work. It is words, moreover, persuasive words – 'pleading a case' – that characterize Esther when Sor Juana explicitly refers to her later in the *Respuesta*. Proving that she knows her Bible, she provides a short list of biblical women in whom she has found models for her 'inclinación a las letras'. Along with Deborah, who gave laws, and the 'sapientisima reina de Saba', we find Esther, praised for her gift of 'persuasión' (76–7). At the same time, while Esther could not have used her gift unless she had dared to enter Ahasuerus's chambers, Sor Juana, far from having entered a room not her own, was in the position of Ahasuerus himself. She suffered someone else's invasion when Fernández published her *critica* without her consent, and with a new title.

Sor Juana acknowledges what the bishop asked her to acknowledge, responding on her own terms to a text stolen from her with another one. But she would remain sensitive to editorial interventions even when she consented to such moves.[169]

---

[169] Sor Juana was generally critical of attempts to re-present her; see her oft-cited sonnet, 'Este, que ves, engaño colorido' (This object which you see – a painted snare), which she spends belittling

The struggle to reclaim her words marks 'To the inimitable pens of Europe' ('Las inimitables plumas'), a *redondilla* or poem of four-line stanzas written in mocking response to the publication of the second volume of her *Obras* in Madrid in 1693.[170] Sor Juana uses it to attack the dedicatory verses composed, in theory, to praise her. Yet, as she frames it, these (male) strangers from across the Atlantic dare to claim that they know her better than Sor Juana knows herself – an implicit return to Fernández's assumption that he has insights into Sor Juana that she lacks. But Sor Juana can afford to be far more direct with these Spanish poets who have given her a body 'composed only of indistinct traces' (mal distintos trazos) that has nothing to do with the real 'her'. The truth is this: 'I am not who you think; your pens have given me a different being . . . I am but as you wish to imagine me' (Non soy yo la que pensáis, / sino es que allá me habéis dado / otro sér en vuestras plumas).[171] As Spanish editors shape this Mexican woman into what they describe on the title page of the *Obras* as the 'decima Musa' or tenth muse, they make her into a *cuerpo* she refuses to acknowledge when it crosses the ocean to arrive in her hands.

The poem was found unfinished among Sor Juana's effects at her death and published in the posthumous third volume of her *Obras* in Madrid in 1700. Frederick Luciani ends his analysis of 'Las Plumas' arguing that Sor Juana's awareness of the bankrupt patronage 'system that called [her poem] into being' meant that she was unable to finish it, and as a result it ultimately 'has nowhere to go'.[172] Despite her many connections to powerful patrons and patronesses in both Mexico and Spain, Sor Juana had little say as to how and which of her words were published, and by whom. Her distance from publishing centres and her cloistered lifestyle militated against her ability to control the paratexts of her works. The bishop had bluntly stated that Sor Juana did not know herself, given her failure to recognize what God had given her, and she needed his help in coming to that recognition. In her late, unfinished poem that has 'nowhere to go', she claims that she knows perfectly well who she is: and that others, in acts of misplaced caring, will be forever mistaken.

Having 'nowhere to go' was the case with another American poet, Anne Bradstreet. We may know Bradstreet best for her poems to her husband, or on the burning of her house in 1666. Or, perhaps, for a phrase from the brief, confessional autobiography, entitled simply 'My Dear Children', composed some ten years before her death when she was pondering what she might say

---

a portrait of her, dismissing it in the final line as a 'cadáver' (corpse) and, ultimately, 'nada'; Juana 2009, pp. 158–9.

[170] Adding to Sor Juana's frustration was surely the fact that the *Carta Atenagórica*, prefaced by Fernández's letter, opened the 1693 edition.

[171] Luciani 2004, p. 140.   [172] Luciani 2004, p. 151.

when the time came: what does she most want her eight children to remember about her? As she writes, when she was eighteen, 'I changed my condition and was married and came into this country, where I found a new world and new manners, at which my heart rose' – a reference to her family's departure from London for Ipswich, Massachusetts, where both her father and her husband were active in setting up a new Puritan community. But, she continues, 'after I was convinced it was the way of God, I submitted to it and joined to the church at Boston'.[173]

Risings and submissions in many ways seem to characterize Bradstreet's life in the 'new world' of Nov-Anglia: particularly in regard to an incident that led to her becoming the first and only woman writer in New England to be published in the seventeenth century. For Bradstreet was utterly unaware that her brother-in-law John Woodbridge carried a manuscript of poems with him to London in 1649, printing them a year later as *The Tenth Muse Lately Sprung Up in America* – absent her name on the title page. Woodbridge introduces the book as 'the Work of a Woman, honoured, and esteemed where she lives' and its 200 pages of poems as 'the fruit but of some few hours, curtailed from her sleep, and other refreshments' rather than time stolen from her husband or children – evidently eager to reassure readers that she is a proper wife and mother.[174] He then confesses, 'I feare the displeasure of no person in the publishing of these Poems but the Authors, without whose knowledge, and contrary to her expect-ation, I have presumed to bring to publick view what she resolved should never in such a manner see the Sun'. His rationale, however, is that he 'found that divers had gotten some scattered papers, affected them well, were likely to have sent forth broken pieces to the Authors prejudice, which I thought to prevent, as well as to pleasure those that earnestly desired the view of the whole' – an echo, it might seem, of the relatively recent First Folio edition of Shakespeare. And the 'whole' is presumably what we have, given us by someone who like Shakespeare's friends is dedicated to recreating entire 'bodies' from fragments. Yet while he claims to have the author in mind as he scurries to protect her reputation, his real concern is 'those that earnestly desired the view of the whole': his readers, titillated by what they have read and eager for more.

Woodbridge is not Sor Juana's bishop demanding that the author recognize herself in pages he publishes but a relative who apparently had a gift manuscript Bradstreet presented to her father, Thomas Dudley. The first words by Bradstreet we encounter in *The Tenth Muse* are indeed addressed to her 'most honoured Father', followed by the four long poems she promises him. She then closes with lines that indicate the end of her 'offering', signing off with her

---

[173] Bradstreet 2019, 'My Dear Children', p. 306.   [174] Bradstreet 2019, 'To the Reader', p. 341.

initials: 'Accept therefore of what is penned, / And all the faults which you shall spy, / Shall at your feet for pardon cry. Your dutiful Daughter, A.B.' (105). As Bradstreet's most recent editor Margaret Thickstun has commented, this seems to be the cover letter – and the close – to a 'formal manuscript collection created for him: a presentation copy'.[175] Yet Woodbridge adds more poems, which were possibly the 'scattered papers' others circulated or sought to publish, among which we have the ambitious but incomplete 'The Four Monarchies', modelled on the poetry of the popular French writer Du Bartas. The fourth such monarchy abruptly breaks off with Lucretia's suicide. Despite the fact that Bradstreet's longest piece in the 1650 volume was clearly unfinished, Woodbridge nonetheless claims to present 'the view of the whole' for eager readers. At the same time, his concern that the (equally unauthorized) publication of 'broken pieces' might work to the 'author's prejudice' suggests that he is doing this ultimately for the author, as an act of charity.[176]

But Bradstreet conceives it as an act of misplaced charity, as she observes in her own *Respuesta*-like poem, 'The Author to Her Book'. Her putative retort to the printed text when it arrived from England opens as follows;

> Thou ill-form'd offspring of my feeble brain,
> Who after birth didst by my side remain
> 'Til snatched from thence by friends, less wise than true,
> Who thee abroad expos'd to public view,
> Made thee in rags, halting to th'press to trudge,
> Where errors were not lessened (all may judge). (265)

Sor Juana did not want to acknowledge the *Carta Atenagórica*, using an analogy arguably more stylized if no less brutal: she hoped that her work would have 'drown'd' rather than to have been pulled out of the waters like Moses. Bradstreet also describes her book as a foundling, as she arguably plays on the term 'expos'd' in its double meaning as orphaned and rendered public. But since the child has come home and she is forced to acknowledge this 'brat' as 'mine own', she is moved to 'thy blemishes amend' – and does what she can 'in better dress to trim', even as she regrets having only 'home-spun cloth' with which to clothe it. The ultimate goal now is to send the book back out – not because she has improved it but because 'thy Mother, she alas is poor, / Which caus'd her thus to send thee out of door'. At least this time, it is the mother's choice.

Such a *congedo* – 'take thy way where yet thou art not known' – suggests that Bradstreet was contemplating a new edition of her poems after she saw what

---

[175] Bradstreet 2019, p. 1.

[176] See Thickstun on publishing norms in mid-seventeenth century England, when it was common 'among persons of social standing to circulate their work in manuscript only, with the poems perhaps appearing in print after their deaths through the efforts of friends'; Bradstreet 2019, p. 1.

Woodbridge wrought. But such a volume never appeared in Bradstreet's lifetime, perhaps because of the destruction of her house, or the author's second thoughts. Either way, after seeing her verses in print, she evidently decided that it was her call, and hers alone, to grant her poetry leave: albeit a decision that emerges from her 'poverty', insinuating that she is no longer able to care for this child. Her book will again become a beggar, dependent on others' charity. Perhaps not coincidentally if in a very different context, at the end of her reflections in 'My Dear Children' Bradstreet invokes the line uttered by Esther when debating whether to enter Ahasuerus's chambers, 'If I perish, let me perish'.[177] Is this her attitude towards her revised and expanded manuscript of poems? At least it will go forth, arguably trespassing into others' domains – that of Du Bartas and other male writers – although this time with the mother's express permission. Only she can give her words licence to speak, no matter how poor she is, as she becomes Ahasuerus and Esther alike.[178]

But such *licenza* was only acted on six years after her death. The 1678 edition, published in Boston, serves as both a re-edition and, in some cases, a revision of the 1650 volume. It also contains several new poems Bradstreet had revised for possible publication as well as other works found by her children after her death 'which she never meant should come to public view', as the title of the book states – thus preparing readers for an act of illegal entry into Bradstreet's private space.[179] The poem to her 'ill-form'd offspring' is situated neither in the section dedicated to the (now-revised) 1650 edition ending on page 235 nor in that entitled 'several poems found in manuscript after her death', beginning on page 237. It is rather situated inbetween the two sections, in a liminal space opened up after the word *FINIS* demarcating the end of the 1650 edition (Figure 4).

Yet we might ask where *Bradstreet* would have placed this daring poem. Why not at the very beginning of the volume, displacing the commendatory verses written by her brother-in-law and the other men whose praises – some distinctly patronizing, some not – usher us into Bradstreet's works, not unlike the dedicatory poems introducing (and per Sor Juana's account, misrepresenting) the Mexican writer to the Spanish world two decades later? Instead, Bradstreet's editors placed this poem to the child who shames her and whom she can never deny, quite literally on the edge. Perhaps intentionally, 'The Author to Her Book' thus becomes

---

[177] Bradstreet 2019, p. 309: Bradstreet admits that she sometimes wonders about the truths of Christianity, given the crises of faith during her time. But she ends her confessional piece to her children pledging, 'Upon this rock Christ Jesus will I build my faith, and if I perish, I perish'. It is a somewhat edgy moment for a Puritan: only at death can one know such things for sure.

[178] See Pender 2012 on how Bradstreet attempted to take back what was taken from her by others.

[179] On the printer John Foster and some of the dubious printing choices he made with the Bradstreet edition, see Bradstreet 1897, pp. xxxvi–xxxix.

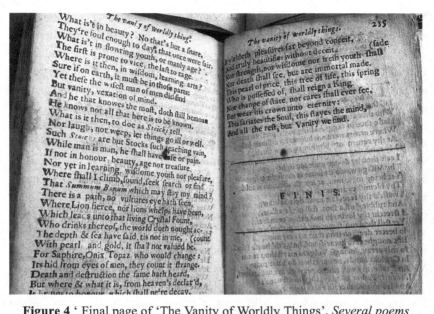

Figure 4 ' Final page of 'The Vanity of Worldly Things', *Several poems compiled with great variety of wit and learning … by a gentlewoman in New-England*, Boston, 1678, pp. 234–5, courtesy Beinecke Library.

Bradstreet's last words before her death, the secular version of the confessional autobiography to her eight children that cites Esther's words before entering Ahasuerus's chamber: if I perish, I perish.

Because this ambivalent blessing of her work appeared in print only after Bradstreet's death – once again, obviously without her consent – it is impossible to know if Bradstreet had ended up circulating a new manuscript of her (revised) works and if this was part of that manuscript, perhaps its point of departure.[180] A little like Horace's final epistle, it asks others to take pity on her work, now sent out with the mother's albeit reluctant blessing of which the 1650 edition was forcibly deprived. And this is the work of a mother, not a *dominus*, who would go on later in life to grieve the deaths of some five grandchildren in addition to a daughter-in-law who died in childbirth. Small wonder that what might have been a poem inaugurating a new volume instead calls attention to the fragility of all mortal things, to their necessary incompleteness and uncertain fate.

---

[180] On the difficulties of knowing which (lost) manuscripts provided the texts for the 1678 edition, see Thickstun: 'No manuscript copies of any of the printed poems – from either volume – survive' (Bradstreet 2019, pp. 26–7).

With the Italian poet Torquato Tasso, we again see professions of compassion for the whole work rather than its pieces – a work put forward as physically embodying the author, despite his utter lack of involvement in its production. Early modern Italy's best-known but most beleaguered poet, Tasso's emotional and mental instabilities landed him for his own safety and that of others in a sixteenth-century version of an asylum in the court of Ferrara, where Tasso had been its brilliant if troubled 'poet-laureate' for almost a decade. If Bradstreet avoided fame, Tasso sought it out, while like Bradstreet he circulated copies of his work in progress in manuscript – sometimes as gift copies but, in most cases, to solicit the opinion of readers he trusted more than himself. This habit of depending on the feedback of others, inquisitors as well as potential patrons, led to his epic masterpiece *Gerusalemme liberata* being disseminated in what John Woodbridge would call 'broken pieces'. And, as a result, in 1580, while Tasso was under lock and key, fourteen of the poem's twenty cantos appeared in print in Venice as *Il Goffredo di M. Torquato Tasso Nuovamente dato in luce.*

No one seems to have been more outraged by this publication than Angelo Ingegneri, a Venetian who would wind up at least twice in prison for various debts, and who was always on the lookout (not unlike Tasso) for supportive, wealthy patrons. Ingegneri dedicated his own edition of the poem to Carlo Emanuele I of Savoia:

> I am that very one who, upon arriving in Parma, found that *Gerusalemme Liberata* completely torn apart (tutta lacera), ... thanks to some who had printed in Venice fourteen discontinuous Canti. Rejected by the eyes of many who, not without disdain, little trusted its integrity (*sanità*), I myself now lead it back to the gaze of the World ([lo] riconduco alla vista del Mondo).[181]

No longer 'concealed under an infinite number of defects in that first, wholly flawed, edition', the poem will hopefully now be protected and favoured by Carlo Emanuele himself: 'Et è V.A. Sereniss. pure, cui tocca protegerla, e favorirla' (Aii.v).

Here too, we see concern for the whole versus the parts, the integral body versus the lacerated one. But in Tasso's case, given the poet's delicate situation with regard to his mental health, Ingegneri's publication of the complete poem becomes a substitution for a woefully lacerated author. This is a more dramatic version of the bishop's conception of a Sor Juana who was theologically unsound, needing to be made whole by his publication of her treatise. Yet in a sonnet following his dedication to Carlo Emanuele, Ingegneri addresses not that author but 'the book': the 'most famous offspring of a famous father ... [but] denied the gift of paternal care'.[182] In the absence of 'paterna cura', friendly compassion ('l'amica pietade') intervenes to ensure that this child will attain a level of fame

---

[181] Tasso 1581, Ai.   [182] Tasso 1581, Biiv.

that will surpass that of all others, Virgil and Homer included. The sonnet ends with this rhetorical question: 'What will you do now with this bright light [of fame], with a true guide?' For finally the *Gerusalemme* has a 'true', reliable, edition, thanks to Ingegneri's paternal care in the absence of Tasso's – an absence that encouraged others to publish incomplete versions of his poem.

Ingegneri introduces this notable lack of fatherly attention in the letter to Carlo Emanuele via an allusion to Tasso's 'strange melancholy' that brought him to the gates of Torino two years earlier, only to be thrown out (ributtato) 'because they didn't trust his sanity' (per non haver fede di Sanità). The word *sanità* or health is used for both the book and the poet, refused entrance into the city at nightfall just as Ingegneri was leaving the church of the Capuccini after Mass. He came to the author's rescue then, and now he does the same for his book, asking a Carlo Emanuele well known for his compassion to assist Tasso in 'such undeserved suffering' (così indegna miseria).

Ingegneri's project worked. The *Goffredo*, as the *Liberata* was originally called, quickly became one of Italy's if not Europe's most popular poems. By 1590, Tasso had been coaxed into collaborating in what would be the work's first illustrated edition, sponsored by a friend of his, one Father Angelo Grillo from Genoa, who was also close to the talented artist Bernardo Castello. In addition to boasting twenty-one engravings, the 1590 edition of the *Gerusalemme liberata* is also the first to contain a dedicatory sonnet by Tasso himself – not to his poem but to Castello. The first three stanzas of Tasso's sonnet are comprised of fairly standard words of praise – the muses prize Castello above all – while the final terzina links the poet to the painter – and hence Tasso to Castello:

> Ma le rivolgi [le serene luci] a' gloriosi Duci,
> Et a' miei versi tu da l'auree stelle
> Muto Poeta di Pittor canoro.[183]

But you turn your eyes from heavenly stars to Glorious Dukes, and to my verses – Mute Poet of a singing painter.

Who is the poet here, who the painter? Tasso plays with a reference to Plutarch's *De gloria Atheniensium* and the line, 'Simonides calls painting silent poetry, and poetry speaking painting'.[184] Tasso turns the speaking painter – i.e., the poet – into the *singing* painter; and while the change is minimal, it implicitly suggests that the real painter Castello has 'muted' more than words: he has silenced music itself. Even as the poem is laudatory, it's noteworthy that Tasso never spoke or wrote again to Angelo Grillo, who had gone to enormous lengths

---

[183] Tasso 1590, p. 6. ('Del Sig. Torquato Tasso').

[184] Plutarch 1936, *De gloria* 3; Vol. 4, p. 501. Plutarch goes on to describe how Thucydides sought to 'make the hearer (as it were) a spectator' (503). My thanks to the reviewer for this reference.

to facilitate the 1590 publication and procure the 'mute poems' of Castello. Apparently denied the chance to weigh in on the final proofs, Tasso would condemn the enterprise in letters written to other associates as he became, perhaps unsurprisingly, increasingly mistrustful of others' handling of his words. Those words included a number of dialogues and poems he had written while locked up in Ferrara, and upon his release in 1586 he set himself up to ensure that what had happened to his epic would never happen again. A typical phrase in his letters of the time is his conviction to publish (*stampare*) all his writing with as much commentary as possible so as to guide his readers in their interpretations.[185] At the same time, he remains keenly aware of the fact that 'printers have neither discretion, nor compassion, nor any conscience whatsoever' ('stampatori non hanno discrezione o pietà o coscienza alcuna').[186] One should never trust those who claim to take care of one's works.

More importantly, Tasso set out to work on a thorough revision of the *Liberata*. His initial dissatisfaction with the text itself was the main reason he hadn't published it. After the pirated editions, he spent a decade revising and rewriting his epic, excising some of its central episodes and adding others to turn his twenty-canto poem into one with twenty-four canti – in line with Homer's two great epics. Ultimately he would disassociate himself not only from Castello's and Grillo's edition but from the *Liberata* itself. The triumphant announcement in April 1593 that his new, revised ('riformato') poem was complete, to be called *Gerusalemme conquistata*, signified a conquering not only of Jerusalem by the Crusaders but of the old *Gerusalemme liberata* by its author. One passage in particular stands out:

> I'm most attached to my new poem – or better, my newly revised poem, as though my intellect had given birth to a new child. I've become alienated from the first child (dal primo sono alieno), like a father of rebellious sons or children suspected of being born out of wedlock. This one is born from my mind, like Minerva born from Jove, as I instill in him both life and spirit itself.[187]

This is the legitimate child, uncontaminated by a woman or, perhaps more importantly, by the body itself, the material corpus that is so difficult to manage, one that can only become malformed through others' unauthorized interventions. The *Conquistata* was not yet published; Tasso goes on in his letter to express his hope that Cinzio Aldobrandini, nephew of the pope, will be the recipient of his new work. Aldobrandini accepted, and the *Conquistata* appeared with a new opening line that

---

[185] One example is a letter from 25 June 1590 where he emphasizes his 'antico disiderio di stampar le mie composizioni'; Tasso 1978, Letter 174 to Antonio Costantini, Vol. 2, p. 370.

[186] Tasso 1978, Letter 175 to Costantini, Vol. 2, p. 373.

[187] Tasso 1978, Letter 202 to Bishop Francesco Panigarola, Vol. 2, p. 400.

features a far bolder version of the poet's voice than that in the original *Gerusalemme*. The *Liberata* begins, Virgil-like, with the phrase 'Canto l'arme pietose e 'l capitano' – I sing of pious arms and the captain – and we are reminded that, in his sonnet to Castello, Tasso would speak of himself as a painter who *sings*. But the *Conquistata* emphasizes the I who does that singing: '*Io* canto l'arme e 'l cavalier sovrano': *I* sing. And yet the *Conquistata* would be essentially a poetic failure, unable to surpass the fame of Tasso's 'alienated' child, already in multiple editions. Tasso edited with a singularly heavy, unimaginative hand, omitting the very ambiguities and much of the richness of the younger, more suggestive *Liberata* – and most readers were, and still are, uninterested in reading to the end. Like Ariosto, he had added new cantos; unlike Ariosto, he had not produced a better, more complete poem.

The *Liberata*, not the *Conquistata*, would continue to have enormous success – as a telling image from the 1745 edition of the poem suggests.[188] Like the Castello edition, this text features a number of illustrations. The final one depicts an outdoor marketplace where the *Liberata* is being sold by a woman sitting next to a sign with the book's price: 'Il suo Prezzo è di Zecchini otto' – 8 zecchini (Figure 5). A young man at the head of the line of prospective buyers asks how

Figure 5 Tasso, *Gerusalemme liberata*, final page, Venice, 1745, courtesy Beinecke Library.

---

[188] I owe the 'discovery' of this image to my former undergraduate student Marlena Hinkle, who wrote an essay on Tasso's inability to relinquish his text. M. Hinkle (2019), 'Altomoro's Surrender: A Warrior's Goodbye', Undergraduate term paper, Yale University.

much the book costs, while a boy brings in more copies to replenish the dwindling supply. On the far right a boat has set sail on the sea that looms beyond, alluding to the journey that Tasso's poem will take as it goes to find new homes. Or as Marlena Hinkle has written, 'As it is sent out to the world, it is of course no longer his. It is being sold to nameless men centuries later and being brought to foreign lands, as the 1745 edition is being brought to Austria', where the poem's dedicatee, the Empress Maria Theresa, resides.[189] Even as Venice remained a republic, its sympathies were very much aligned with the relatively hands-off Hapsburg empire – suggesting why this epic about the First Crusade and its victorious rout of the Muslim occupiers of Jerusalem was dedicated to the Empress herself.

In this distribution of the *Liberata*'s unbound pages to eager readers, some prepared to carry it on horseback all the way to Vienna, there is the implication that this is a brand-new book hot off the press, like the 'daily news', which by the mid-eighteenth century had become a central feature of European life. Tasso's book inspires such curiosity that the man who has just purchased it can barely wait to start reading. Tasso may be long gone, but this send-off suggests that his poem is just as if not more relevant as it was 150 years earlier – thanks in no small part to the works of compassionate editors like Angelo Ingegneri. At the same time, the fact that the book looks like a tombstone in the 1745 edition – 'shaped like a rounded headstone and seemingly protruding from the ground' as Hinkle notes – might suggest that it embodies the corpus of the author himself. The poet who had called himself a 'peregrino errante' or wandering pilgrim in the fourth stanza of the *Liberata* – a line cited by John Florio in his dedicatory letter to Montaigne's *Essais* – is, like Castiglione's English Courtier, finally at rest.[190]

Yet the work that entombs Tasso is not the one he would have chosen to represent him, given his attempt to convince the public of the superiority of his legitimate child, the *poema riformato* that he called the *Conquistata*. Once the author is dead, their sole relationship to their books can only be that of the silent, unmoving tomb. The cover of the third volume of Sor Juana's *Obras* published in Madrid in 1700 announces that Sor Juana lives on, given its title: *Fama y Obras Posthumas del Fenix de Mexico*. But as Frederick Luciani observes, the Phoenix herself commented bitterly on 'seeing her works "entombed" within editorial superstructures not of her design or approval'.[191] A more sombre, less playful editorial sign of rest is found at the end of Anne Bradstreet's posthumous 1678 works, where readers would have

---

[189] Ibid., p. 14.   [190] Tasso 1982, p. 44; I:4.
[191] Luciani 2004, p. 149; the sonnet 'Este que ves' cited previously in this section likens a portrait of Sor Juana to a corpse.

encountered for the first time 'The Author to Her Book', positioned in that awkward but suggestive threshold between Bradstreet's life and death. The latter moment is demarcated by the eleven 'private' poems that Bradstreet never wanted published, and it is followed by a lengthy 'Funeral Elegy upon that Pattern and Patron of Virtue, the truly pious, peerless and matchless Gentlewoman Mrs. Anne Bradstreet', whose 'Heaven-Born Soul' left 'its earthly Shrine, chose its native home, and was taken to its rest' on 16 September 1672. The elegy closes with the words 'Finis and non John Norton' – a minister and mediocre poet intent on reminding us that Bradstreet's 'native home' was not England, where she was born and her first book published, but heaven; the land of Boston where this book is now appearing is only a transitory space. [192] This is the true *finis*. And this, for sure, is not Anne Bradstreet's book. Given the determination of the editors, and perhaps Bradstreet's children, to make her private poems visible to 'publicke view', it never was.

The 1650 edition of Bradstreet that I consulted in the Beinecke Library, however, was at one time most definitely Hannah Peck's book (Figure 6). A century after its publication, a woman reader flipped through the opening dedicatory letter and poems to Bradstreet, past Bradstreet's obsequious dedication to her own father, and to the beginning of her 'serious' body of work, which opens with the 'Four Elements'. Perhaps in an act of recognition as to where Bradstreet's poems *really* began, this is where Hannah Peck decided to claim this text as her own.

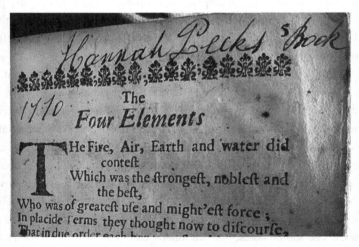

Figure 6 *Tenth muse lately sprung up in America*, London, 1650, opening page of Bradstreet's poems, courtesy Beinecke Library.

---

[192] Bradstreet 2019, p. 355.

Epilogue

> What needs my Shakespeare for his honoured bones,
> The labor of an age in pile'd stones . . .

'My Shakespeare.' So does the young John Milton, excited to have his first poem find its way into print, claim Shakespeare as his own. *His* Shakespeare, rather than his father's, who had written a dedicatory verse for the First Folio edition of Shakespeare's plays. The younger Milton was asked to contribute a verse to the second, 1632 edition. He responded with a sixteen-line 'epitaph' in rhyming couplets, opening with a rhetorical question not so much to the audience as to himself, as he asks why his Shakespeare needs 'pile'd stones', or in short, a tomb, when we have his book – the volume Milton imagines holding in his hands, and which we as readers presumably hold in ours. As though Milton was undoing the 1745 illustration from the close of Tasso's *Gerusalemme liberata*, he exchanges the silent tomb for the flowing sound of 'easy numbers' that issues from the imposing folio, with its equally imposing image of Shakespeare's face. This Shakespeare is not buried in the ground, like Tasso, but is very much alive. And now he is Milton's – even if Milton's name doesn't appear anywhere on the page.

Yet to assert that Shakespeare has no needs is to overlook the very context in which Milton's poem is appearing. Shakespeare needed his friends to pore over the circulating copies of his plays, possibly too busy or careless to do it himself, eager to move to his next masterpiece. He needed friends to edit the plays, organize them, consign them to the press. Milton imagines a world of authorial control and transmission in which there are no mediators, no Condell and Heminge, however good-willed. But once mediators are no longer good-willed, when they thrust themselves onto the scene with nefarious intent, they provoke Milton's wrath, as expressed a dozen years later in one of his most influential pamphlets, *Areopagitica*. The licensing laws long in effect in England had passed from the Archbishop of Canterbury to Parliament, and in the midst of the first round of Civil Wars Parliament moved to create a committee of some twenty licensers or 'examiners' to decide what could be published, and what not. Milton had a personal reason for writing this work, which began as an oration. One of his pamphlets on divorce had been published without such a licence earlier that year, and he had been attacked. At the same time, as George Sabine notes, 'the Stationers' Company petitioned for a stricter enforcement of the licensing law and named Milton as a violator'.[193]

---

[193] Milton 1951, p. vii.

Concerned for his reputation and no doubt his ability to publish in the future, Milton turned private rancour into a defence of the right to determine the fate of one's words after they leave home. Poliziano's Paul had to defend himself against a brash young critic. Milton's critic was the 'patriarchal licenser' with power 'to blot or alter what precisely accords not with the hide-bound humor which he calls his judgment'.[194] That judgement affects not only living authors but the dead as well; and Milton reserves one of his most visceral images for licensors who 'gnaw out the choicest periods of exquisitest books, and commit such a treacherous fraud against the orphan remainders of worthiest men after death' (32). The orphaned text is now needier than ever, given the ability of the licensors to attack not only 'every knowing person alive' but 'the written labors and monuments of the dead'. Shakespeare's Folio entombs, perhaps embalms him, but it is not safe from harm. Seemingly caring far more about the audience than the author, the 'engrosser' intervenes to present a certain version of those author's words to readers who need to be protected from potentially dangerous and incendiary words. Yet it's not the reader the licensors really seek to protect but the state: and Milton nails the reason as to why. Far from being 'absolutely dead things ... [books are] lively and productive as those fabulous dragons teeth' (5–6) – and in the ancient Greek myth of Cadmus, they give birth to warriors. What must be preserved by a nervous government is the status quo – stasis, a word that shares its etymology with 'state'. In discouraging the dissemination of dragons' teeth and new and potentially radical ideas, the licensors want time to stand still.

Hence Milton's call to the 'Lords and Commons of England', a nation 'not slow and dull, but of a quick, ingenious, and piercing spirit; astute to invent, subtle and sinewy to discourse' (43). Two pages later: 'Where there is much desire to learn, there of necessity will be much arguing, much writing, many opinions' (45). And what is needed to sustain 'this flowery crop of knowledge and new light sprung up and yet springing daily in this city' (48) is 'free writing and free speaking' – a freedom quashed by twenty so-called monopolists, seeking to 'bring ... a famine upon our minds again'.

The key word here is 'again'. The move away from monarchy and the Anglican church had already begun by the time of Milton's oration, and the temporary lifting of repressive laws had inspired Milton's hope that England could become the new beacon of Europe, opposed to an Italy and Spain locked hopelessly in a past and present dominated by the Counter-Reformation. Milton had been to Italy in the early 1630s. He was aware that not only had Giordano Bruno's book been burned but his body, a Bruno who had spent significant time in England. He knew of Paolo Sarpi's damning account of the Inquisition. He

---

[194] Milton 1951, pp. 31–2. For Milton, the state should be his governor, not his 'critic'.

had purportedly talked to Galileo, said to be 'a prisoner to [that] Inquisition', as well as other 'learned men' who 'did nothing but bemoan the servile condition into which learning amongst them was brought' (34). All these events attest to what Milton calls the dampening of 'the glory of Italian wits'.[195] Torquato Tasso spent much of the 1570s anticipating the revisions a censor might require in his *Gerusalemme*. Milton is determined that England, in contrast, be a place to discover 'things more remote from our knowledge' (42). His immediate context for this remark involves a metaphor about the difficulty of discerning 'those planets that are oft combust' – literally, closest to the sun – 'and those stars of brightest magnitude that rise and set with the sun. . . The light which we have gained was given us, not to be ever staring on, but by it to discover onward things more remote from our knowledge.' Milton invokes the expansive universes embraced by Galileo and Bruno alike to suggest that one's intellectual quest is ever in motion, ever prepared to explore the hidden and remote in order to 'discern' – a favourite word of Milton's – what is not easily seen.

Only ongoing reading enables us to fashion our capabilities for the discernment of truth, and thus allows the British people to access the 'flowery crop of knowledge' springing up each day – a shift from infinite universes to English gardens. Yet this fertile crop has its parallel in the writer's own work. Texts are ever-moving because an author's ideas are ever-emerging; the beauty of the printing process is that writers can continue to revise while their books are in press, a prerogative that would be taken away if printers were bound to produce only 'the licensed copy': 'And what if the author shall be one so copious of fancy as to have many things well worth the adding come into his mind after licensing, while the book is yet under the press, which not seldom happens to the best and diligentest writers; and that perhaps a dozen times in one book?' (30).[196] Milton didn't have to go far to imagine such an author. He frequently returned to the press to make revisions, and often published multiple versions of a single work. In 1644, he published no fewer than four tracts on divorce. His 1667 *Paradise Lost* consisted of ten books, reappearing five years later with twelve.

Was Milton's compulsive returning to his work – either while it was being printed or after it was released – a way of ensuring that what was left in the world after his departure would not be 'orphan remainders' but a thoroughly updated landscape of his ever-moving thoughts en route to their discernment of truth? Was it a way of holding on to his words, albeit a paradoxical expression of such tenacity: having said goodbye to them, he could not stop thinking about them, and a printed text was simply, literally, a bookmark in an ongoing

---

[195] See Caravale's aptly titled *Libri pericolosi* (*Dangerous Books*) about book censorship and the Inquisition in early modern Italy (2022). On Milton in Italy, see Martin 2017.

[196] Manuscripts were also open texts, as Riddy 2004 points out.

conversation (not unlike Montaigne)? Licensors suppress that conversation by sitting 'upon the birth or death of books, whether they may be wafted into this world or not' (27). In this, they oppose God himself, 'who pours out before us even to a profuseness all desirable things, and gives us minds that can wander beyond all limit and satiety' (26). Milton's mind does nothing if not wander. Once released from that mind, his texts should have the freedom to wander too.

Texts and authors have wandered throughout this *libellus*, symptomatic of their neediness as well as their openness to a world in which they do not always easily fit. Such wandering can be dangerous – for oneself, but also for others. Books spawn men and women like dragons' teeth, and they are not simple replications of the 'author' – just as Milton's Shakespeare is not Shakespeare's Shakespeare (whoever that may have been), and Bruni's Latin Aristotle would not have been recognized by Aristotle. While Milton's passionate treatise helped generate a movement in England that would lead to establishing the first copyright laws in Europe in 1709, his ultimate concern is not the author.[197] Even as Milton seeks liberty for himself to 'utter', his first request is the liberty to know, as we see towards the end of *Areopagitica*: 'Give *me* [italics mine] the liberty to know, to utter; and to argue freely according to conscience, above all liberties' (49). It is, finally, *his* Shakespeare he will attempt to save from the fire or the censor's knife because he, Milton, needs to learn from him. One does the author a grave injustice by preventing his words from coming into the world. But the real injustice is to the reader: to their Sor Juana-like inclination to know.

Authors and readers are not unrelated. The author's freedom is necessarily the reader's, and Milton certainly connects the two, making the one dependent on the other. The author's liberty to intervene in the printing process, to revise and reprint as he sees fit, is essential for the reader desirous of ever-expanding knowledge. Yet unlimited freedom is also a fantasy, and one might see Milton moving towards a romanticism that will embrace the desire for direct, unmediated connections between author and reader, absent the mechanics of scribal copying, print, editing, translation – the work of special *kinds* of readers. Milton was hardly the first to imagine such a thing; Ovid wishes he could *be* his book. But it leaves out the intermediary work that goes into making that book possible – and thus, the fantasies of editors and translators like Bruni, who wants his readers to imagine that Basil himself is speaking. Authors and their intermediaries alike, that is, both engage in the illusion that they are providing readers with experiences of immediacy – although differently.

---

[197] 'The emergence of property in books as a theoretical problem' is only 'shadowy' in *Areopagitica*; see Loewenstein 2002, p. 201.

One might see in Milton's image of an author returning constantly to the press an unwillingness to give up ownership of his work and let it go. Still, as of that very first published poem that appeared in Shakespeare's Second Folio, Milton must have known that should he become one of those 'best and diligentest writers' who factor so heavily in his oration, he would not remain Milton's Milton. He would become someone else's Milton: that of an editor, a translator, or simply a reader who put their initials into a copy of *Paradise Lost* – just as in 1770 Hannah Peck wrote her name in her edition of Anne Bradstreet's poems. But far from being the only one to care for Bradstreet's poems – and we have seen how problematic others' care could be, particularly with respect to Bradstreet herself – she was simply adding her name to an already lengthy list.

References

Agamben, G. (1999). *The End of the Poem: Studies in Poetics*. Trans. D. Heller-Roazen. Stanford: Stanford University Press.

Alexander, G. (2007). 'Prosopopoeia: The Speaking Figure'. In S. Adamson, G. Alexander, and K. Ettenhuber, eds., *Renaissance Figures of Speech*. Cambridge: Cambridge University Press, pp. 97–112.

Alighieri, D. (1984). *The Divine Comedy of Dante Alighieri*. Trans. A. Mandelbaum. Berkeley: University of California Press.

   (1995). *Rime*. Ed. G. Contini. Turin: Einaudi.

   (1999). *Convivio*. Ed. G. Inglese. Milan: BUR.

Allegretti, P. (2006). 'La canzone "montanina": Dante tra Ovidio e Melibeo'. *Dante Studies* 124: 119–36.

Arrigoni, L. (2019). 'Il linguaggio e la morte in Dante. Una nota a Giorgio Agamben'. In G. Giaccardi, ed., *Homo Loquens: Valori e veicoli della parola nel mondo antico e medievale*. Alessandria: Orso, pp. 181–94.

Auerbach, N. (1975). 'Incarnations of the Orphan'. *ELH* 42: 395–419.

Barchiesi, A. (2001). *Speaking Volumes: Narrative and Intertext in Ovid and Other Latin Poets*. London: Duckworth.

Barolini, T. (2006). *Dante and the Origins of Italian Literary Culture*. New York: Fordham University Press.

Bearden, E. (2019). *Monstrous Kinds: Body, Space and Narrative in Renaissance Representations of Disability*. Ann Arbor: University of Michigan Press.

Billanovich, G. (1947). *Petrarca letterato*. Rome: Storia e letteratura.

Blair, A. (2019). 'Erasmus and His Amanuenses'. *Erasmus Studies* 39: 22–49.

Bokser, J. A. (2006). 'Sor Juana's Rhetoric of Silence'. *Rhetoric Review* 25: 5–21.

Bolzoni, L. (2019). *Una meravigliosa solitudine: L'arte di leggere nell'Europa moderna*. Turin: Einaudi.

Boswell, J. (1988). *The Kindness of Strangers: The Abandonment of Children in Western Europe from Late Antiquity to the Renaissance*. New York: Pantheon.

Bradstreet, A. (1678). *Several Poems Compiled with Great Variety of Wit and Learning* .... Boston: Foster.

   (1897). *Poems of Mrs. Anne Bradstreet (1612–1672) Together with Her Prose Remains*. Ed. C. E. Norton. New York: The Duodecimos.

   (2019). *Poems and Meditations*. Ed. M. O. Thickstun. Toronto: Iter.

Brundin, A. (2019). Exhibit: 'Cultures in Translation'. https://exhibitions.lib.cam.ac.uk/hoby/.

Bruni, L. (2004). *Sulla perfetta traduzione*. Ed. P. Viti, Naples: Ligouri.

(1987). 'On the Correct Way to Translate'. Trans. J. Hankins. *The Humanism of Leonardo Bruni*. Binghamton: Center for Medieval and Renaissance Studies, pp. 217–28.

Burke, P. (2002). 'The Courtier Abroad: Or, the Uses of Italy'. In D. Javitch, ed., *Baldessar Castiglione, The Book of the Courtier*. New York: Norton, pp. 388–400.

Butler, S. (2018). 'Things Left Unsaid'. *I Tatti Studies in the Italian Renaissance* 21: 245–74.

Cacciari, M. (2019). *La mente inquieta: Saggio sull'Umanesimo*. Turin: Einaudi.

Caravale, G. (2022). *Libri pericolosi: Censura e cultura italiana in età moderna*. Bari: Laterza.

Castiglione, B. (1561). *The Covrtyer of Covnt Baldessar Castilio*. London: Seres.

(1959). *The Book of the Courtier*. Trans. C. Singleton. New York: Anchor.

(1981). *Il Libro del Cortegiano*. Ed. E. Bonora. Milan: Mursia.

Cervantes, M. (2001). *Don Quixote*. Trans. J. Rutherford. Harmondsworth: Penguin.

(2010). *Don Quijote de la Mancha*. Ed. J. M. L. Megías. Madrid: Castalia Zurbano.

Chartier, R. (1994). *The Order of Books*. Trans. L. Cochrane. Stanford: Stanford University Press.

(2014). *The Culture of Print*. Trans. L. Cochrane. Princeton: Princeton University Press.

Cherchi, P. (2008). *Verso la chiusura*. Bologna: Mulino.

Citroni, M. (1986). 'Le raccomandazioni del poeta: apostrofe al libro e contatto col destinatario'. *Maia* 38: 111–46.

Coldiron, A. (1993). 'Appropriation in Translation'. *The Comparatist* 17: 119–40.

(2015). *Printers without Borders: Translation and Textuality in the Renaissance*. Cambridge: Cambridge University Press.

Colonna, V. (2005). *Sonnets for Michelangelo*. Ed. and trans. A. Brundin. Chicago: University of Chicago Press.

(2021). *Poems of Widowhood: A Bilingual Edition of the 1538 Rime*. Trans. R. Targoff, ed. R. Targoff and T. Tower. New York: Iter.

Cox, J. and Kastan, D. (1997). *A New History of Early English Drama*. New York: Columbia University Press.

Crivelli, T. (2016). 'The Print Traditions of Vittoria Colonna's *Rime*'. In A. Brundin, T. Crivelli, and M. Sapegno, eds., *A Companion to Vittoria Colonna*. Leiden: Brill, pp. 69–139.

Curtius, E. R. (1953). *European Literature and the Latin Middle Ages*. Trans. W. Trask. New York: Harper and Row.

Defaux, G. (2001). *Montaigne et le travail de l'amitié*. Orléans: Paradigme.

De Grazia, M. (1991). *Shakespeare Verbatim: The Reproduction of Authenticity and the 1790 Apparatus*. London: Clarendon.

Desan, P. (2003). 'Les *Essais* comme *freak show* ou Marie de Gournay tutrice d'un enfant monstrueux'. In K. Cameron and L. Wilcott, eds., *Le visage changeant de Montaigne*. Paris: Champion, pp. 307–19.

Desan, P. and Coulombel, A. (1995). *Montaigne in Print: The Presentation of a Renaissance Text: Montaigne's Essais (1580–1995)*. Special issue of *Montaigne Studies*. Chicago: University of Chicago Library.

Donatus, A. (2008). *Life of Virgil*. Trans. D. S. Wilson-Okamura (rev. ed.). www.virgil.org/vitae/a-donatus.htm.

Eden, K. (2001). *Friends Hold All Things in Common*. New Haven: Yale University Press.

Erasmus, D. (1976). *The Correspondence of Erasmus: Letters 298–445*. Trans. R. Mynors and D. Thomson. Toronto: University of Toronto Press.

(2012). *Opus Epistolarum Des. Erasmi Roterodami*, Vol. 2. Ed. P. S. Allen. Oxford: Oxford University Press, pp. 1514–17.

Ferrante, E. (2016). *Frantumaglia*. Trans. A. Goldstein. New York: Europa.

Foucault, M. (1979). 'What Is an Author?' In J. Harari, ed., *Textual Strategies: Perspectives in Post-Structuralist Criticism*. Ithaca: Cornell University Press, pp. 141–60.

Fowler, D. (1989). 'First Thoughts on Closure: Problems and Prospects'. *Materiali e discussioni per l'analisi dei testi classici* 22: 75–122.

Genette, G. (1997). *Paratexts*. Trans. J. Lewin. Cambridge: Cambridge University Press.

Gournay, M. (1998). *Preface to the Essays of Michel de Montaigne*. Ed. and trans. R Hillman and C. Quenel. Tempe: Medieval and Renaissance Texts and Studies.

Green, F. (2012). *Montaigne and the Life of Freedom*. Cambridge: Cambridge University Press.

Greene, T. (1982). *The Light in Troy*. New Haven: Yale University Press.

(1986). *The Vulnerable Text*. New York: Columbia University Press.

Hamilton, J. (2013). *Security*. Princeton: Princeton University Press.

Hexter, R. (2001). 'Ovid in the Middle Ages: Exile, Mythographer, and Lover'. In B. Boyd, ed., *Brill's Companion to Ovid*. Leiden: Brill, pp. 413–42.

(1986). *Ovid and Medieval Schooling: Studies in Medieval School Commentaries on Ovid's Ars amatoria, Epistulae ex Ponto, and Epistulae Heroidum*. Munich: Arbeo-Gesellschaft.

Hoffman, G. (1998). *Montaigne's Career*. Oxford: Clarendon.

Horace. (2004). *Odes and Epodes*. Trans. N. Rudd. Cambridge, MA: Harvard University Press.

(2014). *Satires; Epistles; The Art of Poetry*. Trans. H. R. Fairclough. Cambridge, MA: Harvard University Press.

Jardine, L. (2014). *Erasmus, Man of Letters*. Princeton: Princeton University Press.

Jerome. (2000–). Preface to Samuel and Kings. https://earlychurchtexts.com/main/jerome/preface_helmeted_to_kings.shtml.

Johns, A. (1998). *Nature of the Book: Print and Knowledge in the Making*. Chicago: University of Chicago Press.

Juana Inés de la Cruz, S. (2005). *Sor Juana: Selected Writings*. Trans. P. K. Rappaport. New York: Paulist Press.

(2009). *The Answer/La Respuesta*. Ed. and trans. E. Arenal and A. Powell. New York: Feminist Press.

Keen, C. (2009). "'Va', mia canzone": Textual Transmission and the *Congedo* in Medieval Exile Lyrics'. *Italian Studies* 64(2): 183–97.

(2014). 'Ovid's Exile and Medieval Italian Literature: The Lyric Tradition'. In J. Miller and C. Newlands, eds., *Handbook to the Reception of Ovid*. London: Wiley and Sons, pp. 144–60.

La Boétie, E. and Bonnefon, P. (2007). *The Politics of Obedience*. Montreal: Blackrose.

Levin, J. (1984). 'Sweet, New Endings: A Look at the Tornada in the Stilnovistic and Petrarchan Canzone'. *Italica* 61(4): 297–311.

Loewenstein, J. (2002). *The Author's Due: Printing and the Prehistory of Copyright*. Chicago: University of Chicago Press.

Lombardi, E. (2018). *Imagining the Woman Reader in the Age of Dante*. Oxford: Oxford University Press.

Lowry, M. (1979). *The World of Aldus Manutius: Business and Scholarship in Renaissance Venice*. Ithaca: Cornell University Press.

Luciani, F. (2004). *Literary Self-Fashioning in Sor Juana Inés de la Cruz*. Lewisburg: Bucknell University Press.

Manutius, A. (2017). *Humanism and the Latin Classics*. Ed. and trans. J. N. Grant. Cambridge, MA: Harvard University Press.

Marcozzi, L. (2015). 'Making the *Rerum vulgarium fragmentum*'. In A. Ascoli and U. Falkeid, eds., *Cambridge Companion to Dante*. Cambridge: Cambridge University Press, pp. 51–62.

Marino, J. (2013). *Owning William Shakespeare: The King's Men and Their Intellectual Property*. Philadelphia: University of Pennsylvania Press.

Martial. (1968). *Epigrams*. 3 vols. Trans. W. Ker. Cambridge, MA: Harvard University Press.

(1993). *Epigrams*. 3 vols. Trans. D. R. Shackleton Bailey. Cambridge, MA: Harvard University Press.

Martin, C. (2017). *Milton's Italy: Anglo-Italian Literature, Travel, and Connections in Seventeenth-Century England*. New York: Routledge.

Martinez, R. (2009). 'Places and Times of the Liturgy from Dante to Petrarch'. In Z. Barański and T. Cachey Jr. , eds., *Petrarch and Dante: Anti-Dantism, Metaphysics, Tradition*. Notre Dame: Notre Dame University Press, pp. 320–70.

McCarter, S. (2015). *Horace between Freedom and Slavery: The First Book of Epistles*. Madison: University of Wisconsin Press.

McDonald, R. (1993). 'An Incredible Graph: Sor Juana's *Respuesta*'. *Revista Canadiense de Estudios Hispánicos* 17(2): 297–318.

McGowan, M. (2005). 'Ovid and Poliziano in Exile'. *International Journal of the Classical Tradition* 12: 25–45.

Merrim, J. (1999). *Early Modern Women's Writing and Sor Juana Inés de la Cruz*. Nashville: Vanderbilt University Press.

Milton, J. (1951). *Areopagitica and Of Education*. Ed. G. Sabine. New York: Wiley-Blackwell.

Minnis, A. (2010). *Medieval Theory of Authorship*, 2nd ed. Philadelphia: University of Pennsylvania Press.

Montaigne, M. (1598). *Les Essais de Michel seigneur de Montaigne*. Paris: Abel l'Angelier.

   (1603). *The Essayes, or Morall, Politike and Millitarie Discourses of Lo: Michaell de Montaigne*. London: Edward Blount.

   (1613). *Essayes written in French by Michael Lord of Montaigne* .... London: Blount.

   (1960). *The Complete Works of Michel de Montaigne*. Trans. D. Frame. New York: Doubleday.

   (1962). *Essais*. 2 vols. Ed. M.Rat. Paris: Garnier

Mordine, M. (2010). '*Sine me, liber, ibis*: The poet, the book and the reader in *Tristia* 1.1'. *Classical Quarterly* 60: 524–44.

Murphy, A., ed. (2000). *The Renaissance Text: Theory, Editing, Textuality*. Manchester: Manchester University Press.

Nagel, A. (1997). 'Gifts for Michelangelo and Vittoria Colonna'. *The Art Bulletin* 79(4): 647–68.

Najemy, J. (2006). *A History of Florence: 1200–1575*. Malden, MA: Blackwell.

Navarrete, I. (1994). *Orphans of Petrarch: Poetry and Theory in the Spanish Renaissance*. Berkeley: University of California Press.

Newlands, C. (1997). 'The Role of the Book in *Tristia* 3.1'. *Ramus* I: 57–79.

Newman, K. and Tylus, J., eds. (2015). *Early Modern Cultures of Translation*. Philadelphia: University of Pennsylvania Press.

Oliensis, E. (1995). 'Life after Publication: Horace, *Epistles* 1:20'. *Arethusa* 28 (2/3): 209–24.

Orgel, S. (1996). 'What Is an Editor?' *Shakespeare Studies* 24: 23–9.

(2023). *The Idea of the Book and the Creation of Literature*. Oxford: Oxford University Press.

Ovid. (1996). *Tristia/Ex Ponto*. Trans. A. L. Wheeler, rev. G. P. Goold. Cambridge, MA: Harvard University Press.

Pender, P. (2012). *Early Modern Women's Writing and the Rhetoric of Modesty*. New York: Palgrave Macmillan.

Peraino, J. (2011). *Giving Voice to Love: Song and Self-Expression from the Troubadours to Guillaume de Machaut*. Oxford: Oxford University Press.

Petrarch, F. (1979). *Petrarch's Lyric Poems: The Rime Sparse and Other Lyrics*. Ed. and trans. R. Durling. Cambridge, MA: Harvard University Press.

(2017). *Res Seniles*. Ed. Silvia Rizzo, 4 vols. Florence: Le Lettere.

Petrucci, A. (1995). *Writers and Readers in Medieval Italy*. Ed. and trans. C. Radding. New Haven: Yale University Press.

Pettegree, A. (2010). *The Book in the Renaissance*. New Haven: Yale University Press.

Pfeiffer, D. (2022). *Authorial Personality and the Making of Renaissance Texts*. Oxford: Oxford University Press.

Phillips, M. M. (1964). *The 'Adages' of Erasmus*. Cambridge: Cambridge University Press.

Pirovani, D., ed. (2012). *Poeti del Dolce Stil Novo*. Rome: Salerno.

Plato (2005). *Euthyphro . . . Phaedrus*. Trans. H. N. Fowler. Cambridge, MA: Harvard University Press.

Plutarch. (1936). *Were the Athenians More Famous in War or in Wisdom?* In *Moralia*, Vol. IV, trans. F. C. Babbitt. Cambridge, MA: Harvard University Press, pp. 489–527.

Polezzi, L. (2012). 'Translation and Migration'. *Translation Studies* 5(3): 345–56.

Poliziano (1952). 'Orazione su Quintiliano e sulle "Selve" di Stazio'. In E. Garin, ed., *Prosatori latini del Quattrocento*. Milan: Ricciardi, pp. 872–965.

(2000). *L'Orfeo del Poliziano*. Ed. A. Tissoni-Benvenuti. Rome: Antenore.

(2004). *Silvae*. Ed. and trans. C. Fantazzi. Cambridge, MA: Harvard University Press.

(2006). *Letters, Books I–IV*. Ed. and trans. S. Butler. Cambridge, MA: Harvard University Press.

(2012). *Stanze/Orfeo/Rime*. Ed. D. Puccini. Milan: Garzanti.

(2019). *Greek and Latin Poetry*. Ed. and trans. P. Knox. Cambridge, MA: Harvard University Press.

Pozen, D. (2003). 'Friendship without the Friend: The Many Meanings of La Boétie for Montaigne'. *Comitatus: A Journal of Medieval and Renaissance Studies* 34: 135–49.

Prodan, S. (2014). *Michelangelo's Christian Mysticism*. Cambridge: Cambridge University Press.

Putnam, G. (1962). *Books and Their Makers during the Middle Ages*, 2 vols. New York: Hillary House.

Richardson, B. (2018). 'The Social Transmission of Translations in Renaissance Italy: Strategies of Dedication'. In A. Rizzi, ed., *Trust and Proof in Renaissance Translation*. Leiden: Brill, pp. 13–32.

Riddy, F. (2004). '"Publication" before Print: The Case of Julian of Norwich'. In J. Crick and A. Walsham, eds., *The Uses of Script and Print 1300–1700*. Cambridge: Cambridge University Press, pp. 29–49.

Rizzi, A. (2017). *Vernacular Translation in Quattrocento Italy*. Turnout: Brepols.

(2018). 'Monkey Business: *Imitatio* and Translators' Visibility in Renaissance Europe'. In A. Rizzi, ed., *Trust and Proof: Translators in Renaissance Print Culture*. Leiden: Brill, pp. 33–61.

Sannazaro, J. (1966). *Arcadia and Piscatorial Eclogues*. Trans. R. Nash. Detroit: Wayne State University Press.

(2013). *Arcadia*. Ed. C. Vecce. Rome: Carocci.

Shakespeare, W. (1623). *Mr. William Shakespeares Comedies, Tragedies, & Histories*. London: Iaggard and Blount.

Sherman, W. (2011). 'The Beginning of "The End": Terminal Paratext and the Birth of Print Culture'. In H. Smith and L. Wilson, eds., *Renaissance Paratexts*. Cambridge: Cambridge University Press, pp. 65–88.

Sobecki, S. (2019). *Last Words: The Public Self and the Social Author in Late Medieval England*. Oxford: Oxford University Press.

Stallybrass, P. (2011). 'Afterword'. In H. Smith and L. Wilson, eds., *Renaissance Paratexts*. Cambridge: Cambridge University Press, pp. 204–19.

Stock, B. (1990). *Listening for the Text: On the Uses of the Past*. Philadelphia: University of Pennsylvania Press.

Stroup, S. (2010). *Catullus, Cicero, and a Society of Patrons: The Generation of the Text*. Cambridge: Cambridge University Press.

Tasso, T. (1590). *La Gierusalemme liberata di Torquato Tasso*. Genova, 1590.

(1745). *Gerusalemme liberata*. Venice: Albrizzi.

(1978). *Lettere*. Ed. E. Mazzali, 2 vols. Turin: Einaudi.

(1982). *Gerusalemme liberata*. Ed. F. Chiappelli. Milan: Rusconi.

Taylor, M. (2018). *Last Works: Lessons in Leaving*. New Haven: Yale University Press.

Theocritus. (1989). *The Idylls*. Trans. R. Wells. Harmondsworth: Penguin.

Tylus, J. (2023). 'Listening for the Ending'. In S. Powrie and G. Zak, eds., *Textual Communities, Textual Selves*. Toronto: University of Toronto Press, pp. 215–34.

van Groningen, B. A. (1963). 'ΕΚΔΟΣΙΣ'. *Mnemosyne* 16(1): 1–17.

van Orden, K. (2013). *Music, Authorship, and the Book in the First Century of Print*. Berkeley: University of California Press.

Virgil. (2006). *Eclogues. Georgics. Aeneid I–VI*. Trans. H. R. Fairclough, rev. G. P. Goold. Cambridge, MA: Harvard University Press.

Watkin, W. (2010). *The Literary Agamben: Adventures in Logopoiesis*. London: Continuum.

Williams, G. (2001). 'Ovid's Exilic Poetry: Worlds Apart'. In B. Weiden, ed., *Brill's Companion to Ovid*. Leiden: Brill, pp. 337–81.

Wray, G. (2017). 'Challenging Theological Authority'. In E. Gergmann and S. Schlau, eds., *Routledge Research Companion to the Works of Sor Juana Inés de la Cruz*. London: Taylor and Francis, pp. 133–9.

Wyatt, M. (2005). *The Italian Encounter with England: A Cultural Politics of Translation*. Cambridge: Cambridge University Press.

Zak, G. (2010). *Petrarch's Humanism and Care of the Self*. Cambridge: Cambridge University Press.

Zanker, A. (2018). *Greek and Latin Expressions of Meaning: The Classical Origins of a Modern Metaphor*. Munich: Beck.

Acknowledgements

Countless friends and colleagues have helped with the gestation of this book, and were more space allotted me this *congedo* would be much longer! But Sarah Prodan as well as Gur Zak and Sarah Powrie deserve special thanks for welcoming me to conferences at the University of Toronto in, respectively, 2015 and 2019, when some of these ideas were first being fleshed out. Since then I have benefited enormously from conversations with three cohorts of students who have taken variations of a course on 'saying goodbye', and with the many scholars whose work is cited in these pages. As always, my biggest thanks go to William Klein for his patience, love, and support. I am also grateful to series editors Jonathan and John, to the two anonymous reviewers, and to Vibhu Prathima Palanisame and the Cambridge editorial staff for all their help.

I dedicate this libellus to Stephen Orgel, whose generosity,
intellectual verve, and elegant, no-nonsense prose have provided endless fonts
of inspiration for four decades.

Cambridge Elements ⬓

The Renaissance

John Henderson
Birkbeck, University of London, and Wolfson College, University of Cambridge

John Henderson is Emeritus Professor of Italian Renaissance History at Birkbeck, University of London, and Emeritus Fellow of Wolfson College, University of Cambridge. His recent publications include *Florence Under Siege: Surviving Plague in an Early Modern City* (2019), and *Plague and the City*, edited with Lukas Engelmann and Christos Lynteris (2019), and *Representing Infirmity: Diseased Bodies in Renaissance Italy*, edited with Fredrika Jacobs and Jonathan K. Nelson (2021). He is also the author of *Piety and Charity in Late Medieval Florence* (1994); *The Great Pox: The French Disease in Renaissance Europe*, with Jon Arrizabalaga and Roger French (1997); and *The Renaissance Hospital: Healing the Body and Healing the Soul* (2006). Forthcoming publications include a Cambridge Element, *Representing and Experiencing the Great Pox in Renaissance Italy* (2023).

Jonathan K. Nelson
Syracuse University Florence

Jonathan K. Nelson teaches Italian Renaissance Art at Syracuse University Florence and is research associate at the Harvard Kennedy School. His books include *Filippino Lippi* (2004, with Patrizia Zambrano); *Leonardo e la reinvenzione della figura femminile* (2007), *The Patron's Payoff: Conspicuous Commissions in Italian Renaissance Art* (2008, with Richard J. Zeckhauser), *Filippino Lippi* (2022); and he co-edited *Representing Infirmity. Diseased Bodies in Renaissance Italy* (2021). He co-curated museum exhibitions dedicated to Michelangelo (2002), Botticelli and Filippino (2004), Robert Mapplethorpe (2009), and Marcello Guasti (2019), and two online exhibitions about Bernard Berenson (2012, 2015). Forthcoming publications include a Cambridge Element, *Risks in Renaissance Art: Production, Purchase, Reception* (2023).

Assistant Editor
Sarah McBryde, *Birkbeck, University of London*

Editorial Board
Wendy Heller, *Scheide Professor of Music History, Princeton University*
Giorgio Riello, *Chair of Early Modern Global History, European University Institute, Florence*
Ulinka Rublack, *Professor of Early Modern History, St Johns College, University of Cambridge*
Jane Tylus, *Andrew Downey Orrick Professor of Italian and Professor of Comparative Literature, Yale University*

About the Series
Timely, concise, and authoritative, Elements in the Renaissance showcases cutting-edge scholarship by both new and established academics. Designed to introduce students, researchers, and general readers to key questions in current research, the volumes take multi-disciplinary and transnational approaches to explore the conceptual, material, and cultural frameworks that structured Renaissance experience.

Cambridge Elements ☰

The Renaissance

Elements in the Series

Printed in the United States
by Baker & Taylor Publisher Services